Piaget
for
teachers

Piaget
for
teachers

HANS G. FURTH

*The Catholic University
of America*

PRENTICE-HALL, INC. *Englewood Cliffs, N.J.*

PRENTICE-HALL INTERNATIONAL, INC., *London*
PRENTICE-HALL OF AUSTRALIA, PTY. LTD., *Sydney*
PRENTICE-HALL OF CANADA, LTD., *Toronto*
PRENTICE-HALL OF INDIA PRIVATE LIMITED, *New Delhi*
PRENTICE-HALL OF JAPAN, INC., *Tokyo*

contents

preface

With this small book I fulfill a promise made when I sent the publisher *Piaget and Knowledge: Theoretical Foundation* (1969). I admitted then that the book I had originally planned would discuss educational implications of Piaget's theory. However, the book turned into a lengthy and detailed probing of Piaget's theory of knowledge; this was not the kind of material that offered teachers a suitable introduction to practical applications. Thus, having written the theoretical book and seen it published by Prentice-Hall, I lost no time in writing these few pages. The reader—whom I address in letter form as teacher, in the hope that any adult will gladly share the privilege of being teacher to the child—will, I hope, sense the twin urgencies which prompted my writing. I refer to the critical situation in our schools and to the veritable educational revolution which an enlightened acceptance of Piaget's theory could bring about.

While little need be said about the first point, I should state at once that the main purpose of the book is to make Piaget's work better known among educators. I attempt to present, concisely and clearly, key aspects of Piaget's philosophy, theory, and findings that have immediate relevance and critical implications for the educational process. Piaget's direct contribution to education will not be found in specific methods for teaching subject matter. But Piaget may well add a valid theory to effective methods that many educators have developed for particular fields of educational content. For this reason I address myself particularly to the many teachers who realize full well the problems with education as it is and who work intelligently and tirelessly within an educational structure that often does not provide the help and guidance which individual teachers could expect. I am also thinking of those who actively participate in imaginative programs aimed at this or that special curriculum need. But these teachers, like so many others in civic, administrative, and political positions, may still be looking for a generalized rationale, a broadly based theory of how intelligence develops in the child and what an educational system can best do to facilitate that development. When teachers have a theoretical understanding of why they do the things that seem to "work" or "feel right," they will have more than intuitive wisdom on which to base effective methods of teaching.

I could perhaps have written about Piaget's theory and about thinking games without mentioning reading and language at all. I could have left the critical observations implicit, as Piaget has done, rather than coming into the open and saying the unthinkable. Piaget himself is not personally involved in education and therefore has had no need to go out of his way to criticize existing school structures. But I am involved in children's education, and I write for the benefit of those whose life work is committed to this end. For me to say that the traditional focus of elementary schools—reading and writing—needs to be supplemented by an additional emphasis on intellectual growth would be to offer a half-truth which for practical purposes would take the fuel from the fire. You, the reader, would misinterpret Piaget— simply in order to make his ideas congruous with your tacit theoretical and practical ideas about children's learning. Moreover, any practical application to foster intellectual growth would at best become an added school program, a luxury suffered half willingly by a school administration that is going about its usual business of teaching reading and writing. No, it would not be honest for me to present Piaget to you teachers in such an implicit fashion.

Let me be quite blunt. Reading and writing should have no more emphasis or focus in a child's life in early school grades than toilet training has in an infant's first years. In Freud's Vienna, into which I was born, the main task of the bourgeois mother seems to have been to get the children out of diapers by their first birthdays. Society called a failure the mother or child who did not succeed at this feat. In the freer atmosphere of the United States of America, my wife and I are permitted to have our children in diapers well beyond their first birthdays without experiencing feelings of failure. Nor, for that matter, do we expect our children to become less well toilet-trained grownups than their Viennese forebears. Seriously, while the written word is the means par excellence for expanding a mature intelligence, the early pressure on reading must be exposed not merely as contributing little or nothing to intellectual development but, in many cases, as seriously interfering with it.

I do not hide the fact that I am enlisting the popularity of Piaget's name in the cause of changing a system of early education that is psychologically unsound. But if Piaget's theory of development has any validity, surely its first application should be in early education. If the formal teaching of reading turns out to be working against the development of the intelligent person, we should seriously consider whether, as educators, we have asked the proper questions. We are searching continually for new methods of teaching reading without ever asking whether reading is the appropriate focus of early education. Instead, I suggest that the *spontaneously growing intelligence* of the child should be the focus of grade-school activities and that all else should be subordinated to this priority. And I propose Piaget's view of the developing intelligence as a viable alternative to other views of learning currently in favor.

A wholehearted and consistent application of Piaget's theory has potentially so many advantages that it is to be hoped that some innovative school will "take the risk" of putting into practice the ideas of this book. Not the least advantage would be that the use of oral and written language will not be divorced from active thinking. One thing our society needs more than anything else is the intelligent use of words. The accent here is on human ineligence and human knowing. Traditionally, we have assumed that language is a major source that feeds the developing intelligence. Piaget objects to this view unequivocally. Applying Piaget's work to early education, I cannot do less than object to the customary untimely emphasis on reading and language.

I mention here the names of persons who have provided life examples of teaching for thinking and whose classes I observed and will describe in Part Two. Linda Jenstrom at the Center for Research in

Thinking and Language of Catholic University helped for some years with the symbol-picture logic (Letter 8). Caryl and Sydney Wolff participated in the Thinking Laboratory at the West Virginia School for the Deaf in Romney, West Virginia (Letter 9). Henry Ray of the Warminster Schools in Pennsylvania demonstrated his use of photo-technology to encourage visual thinking (Letter 9). Carol Even and Norman Gevanthor from the Arena Stage in Washington introduced me to the drama technique as applied to early schools (Letter 10). Jim Campbell at P.S. 144, New York City, gave me some ideas concerning social thinking (Letter 11). Jack Blatt originated the method of teaching strings at Woodstock, Virginia (Letter 12). Darrell Boyd Harmon from Austin, Texas, and the University of Wisconsin provided me with data and a new perspective on the physiological development of the visual mechanism (Letter 13). My sincere thanks to them, and to colleagues and students with whom I had the privilege of sharing my views.

H.G.F.

Washington, D. C.

Piaget
for
teachers

HANS G. FURTH

foreword

I am pleased and honored to be invited to contribute a foreword to this excellent and attractive little book, in which I hope you are about to invest your thoughtful attention. It is an important book because it goes directly to a question so fundamental that much of educational policy and practice must inevitably pivot upon the answer. This question could scarcely have been asked two decades ago; but now, as new evidence comes in, it claims our attention with increasing intensity.

Put briefly, the question is: When a child begins school, must we take his "intelligence" (as indicated, say, by an IQ test) as something fixed and immutable, representing what the child is—and must we therefore settle for equipping him with whatever competences such an intelligence is capable of bearing? Or is it possible to assume that the ability to think and to learn is itself a growing thing and therefore cultivable? In the first case we must content ourselves with whatever harvest of knowledge and skill we can garner from a mind "naturally" either fertile or barren. In the second, it may be wiser to work at preparing the seed bed.

A growing body of evidence, in the direction of hope, is coming in from many scholars. From no other source has it come so revealingly as from the dedicated life-work of Jean Piaget. For Piaget's painstaking studies of growing children have given us a new conception of the way thinking grows.

Now Professor Furth, in thirteen charming and sensible letters to teachers, interprets what Piaget's discoveries can mean to our schools. Himself a recognized scholar in psychology, he has the added advantage of first-hand intimacy with the work of Piaget, with whom he worked for a year, and first-hand acquaintance with schools and teachers. And he has the ability to write simply and directly.

On first glance you may be inclined to think that Furth's notion of "a school for thinking" is but a new version of Dewey's progressive education with its accent on experience and action. Although there may be similarities in objectives, Furth builds upon the deep insights of Piaget's half-century of work with children in order to put educational practice on a new psychological foundation.

You must not expect this book to be easy going at every step. The profound insights of a great mind like Piaget's do not nestle down instantly into other minds. Furthermore, his thinking is so far outside our traditional frame of reference that our old preoccupations keep getting in the way. No matter how clearly an interpreter simplifies things for us, it takes effort to comprehend.

But Furth is a good teacher. In Part One of the book, where he is explicating Piaget, he moves a short step at a time, and keeps going back to build the earlier material into what comes later. What may appear first as a brief, hard-to-comprehend definition will keep reappearing with fresh examples and added dimensions. If you will trust his guidance, you will soon find "hard" ideas coming rather naturally.

And when, in Part Two, the author shifts to practical suggestions of things to do, you will feel quite at home with him. Piaget's understanding of how a child's thinking grows will flow naturally into understanding of how you can help. Of course, Furth can only sketch some realistic examples and hint at others; you must go on from there. But that ought to be a stimulating thing to do. As Furth might say at the end of one of his letters, I wish you every success.

Fred T. Wilhelms

Executive Secretary,
Association for Supervision and
Curriculum Development

what is the problem?

Dear Teacher:

It seems hardly necessary to belabor the fact that our educational system is in serious and ever increasing trouble. This trouble can be measured in terms of low reading levels, scholastic failures, discipline problems, dropouts, and delinquency. We know that for each child who falls into one of these categories, this is only the beginning of failure. It is not easy to obtain reliable statistics on the number of children as young as grade four who have never experienced the thrill of an intellectual adventure along the path that leads to scholarly success. The fact is that a staggering number of young children, barely ten years old, have already turned their backs on intellectual and social growth, have given up on society and its institutions, and each year come to increase the swelling number of maladapted persons in our society.

The early years of elementary schooling are the last chance, as it were, to give these youngsters a spontaneous experience of success, sanctioned by society, before they have reached the age of reflective awareness. Lacking this experience, they come to regard themselves as failures both in their own eyes and in the eyes of society. Remediation, rehabilitation, redoing—these remedies are in store for a few of them from a benevolent society which is perhaps not as unkind as some would judge, but which is

1

quite irrational in not providing appropriate opportunities for mediation, for habilitation, for doing the appropriate thing when the time is ripe, when chances of success are high and when financial expenditure would be relatively small.

We are but scratching the surface with our piecemeal efforts—a new reading program here, a new language arts program there, diagnostic testing in one school, perceptual training projects in another. These activities are like ripples on the ocean of an elementary-school system that is unsuited and unhealthy for a vast majority of our children. We need a new philosophy that does not merely ameliorate or add to existing structures. We must start from the ground up in a professional, rational manner and ask ourselves what kind of school is psychologically and socially suitable for the children of today.

Lest you think me an idle dreamer, unwilling to face reality, I hasten to assure you of my full realization that, of all institutions, our schools have been rightly regarded as the most conservative, the least changed over the years, and the most complex agency in terms of social, political, professional, and civic investment. I do not know what forces will change the schools. But I know that somebody has to say somewhere what ought to be done. I do not find that what has been said so far is said in as clear and loud a voice as it should be.

If there is any attempt to put the blame on someone, it is first of all directed at my own profession of psychology, which has failed to give the lead one could expect from it. The community at large, and parents in particular, it is often said, would not stand for any radical change and would oppose the introduction of a new educational structure. In the face of this obstacle, let me make two observations. First, who has told the parents what children should do in schools? Do parents tell pediatricians what medicine to give a child? If parents now insist on a certain school curriculum, is it possible that we experts have sold this particular idea to them? Second, most parents are, I believe, reasonable. If we experts are deeply convinced of our position, we can probably persuade the layman. After all, even though politics has its hand in education, there is a big difference between the two disciplines. In politics there simply is not one right and one wrong way, for we have scant possibility of controlled observations that can lead to reasonable agreement. But in education there is the possibility of stating at least some things with the full conviction of a scientific opinion.

What I propose on the matter of early schools is, therefore, not vague speculation on my part. I speak as a responsible scientist, and I am ready to supply supporting empirical evidence from observations, experiments, and theory.

Briefly, I propose these seven points:

1. Reading and writing proficiency are most valuable and desirable skills. In the higher grades they are the principal medium through which knowledge is imparted and articulated.

2. Knowledge can be viewed under a specific and a general aspect. As specific knowledge or learning, it has to do with particular information and particular rules pertaining to a specialized, circumscribed area of study—for example, biology, law, history, literature. As general knowledge, it relates to the overall capacity to acquire and apply special knowledge. We may call this capacity *intelligence* —with the proviso that it not be equated with an IQ score. When intelligence is particularly active in the child's behavior, let us call this activity *thinking.* One can easily separate *thinking* activities that bring the child's intelligence to bear on a particular problem from those *learning* activities in the early grades that are predominantly acquiring new information by memory or description.

3. The age range of five to ten years, roughly kindergarten through grade four, constitutes the establishment of what Piaget calls "operational" intelligence. It is during this time that the stable concepts of space, time, relations, classes, combinations, etc., become available to the child, and it is precisely these broad concepts that are the stuff of general knowledge or intelligence. These general concepts of the developing intelligence evolve whether the child goes to school or not, because they are not dependent upon specific instruction. Moreover, these concepts are the base on which the learning of any special knowledge must rest if it is to be anything more than rote memory.

4. Although the development of intelligence proceeds spontaneously, it can be helped or hindered by the environment. There is ample suggestive evidence that the highly industrialized and technological world into which children are born is far from an ideal environment for the growing intelligence. It is hard, if not impossible, for the child to apply his spontaneous curiosity to a television set, when only an expert can understand how it works, or to vegetables in a tin when he has never observed them growing. Moreover, if there is no social encouragement toward intellectual curiosity, the deadening effect of an environment that is not understood becomes doubly evident. In

short, many children enter school, if not with a crippled intelligence, at least with an intelligence that is not well nourished.

The main points of my argument follow.

5. Assuming that many children who come to school are intellectually impoverished but still have enough internal motivation to grow intellectually—as is shown by the fact that their intellects will continue to grow with or without school—what, in effect, is the school offering the child? This is the message he gets: "Forget your intellect for a while, come and learn to read and write; in five to seven years' time, if you are successful, your reading will catch up with the capacity of your intellect, which you are developing in spite of what we offer you." Mark well these twin conditions: learn reading and forget your intellect. These two things go hand in hand. The average five- to nine-year-old child from any environment is unlikely, when busy with reading or writing, to engage his intellectual powers to any substantial degree. Neither the process of reading itself nor the comprehension of its easy content can be considered an activity well suited to developing the mind of the young child.

A school that in the earliest grades focuses primarily on reading cannot also focus on thinking. It must choose to foster one or the other. Historically, it has chosen reading. Undoubtedly, it once could be tacitly assumed that a child's thinking had developed adequately before he entered school and continued to do so outside of school. These assumptions were perhaps not altogether ill-founded. Schooling in the past was the prerogative of a special class and only gradually broadened its base to include a school-minded and school-ambitious citizenship within a relatively stable social and physical environment that was generally conducive to spontaneous intellectual growth. But today these assumptions are largely irrelevant for a large segment of our population.

6. Reading, like any specialized learning, presupposes a motivation primarily of a different sort from the motivation underlying a child's capacity to think. Reading is learned because the child wants to please his parents, to imitate his peers, or to explore the contents of books. Thus, the motivation of reading lies outside the reading process; it is *extrinsic.* The reading difficulties of an ordinary eight- or nine-year-old child are most likely due to lack of motivation or to faulty learning habits and should not be attributed to lack of intelligence.

On the other hand, the motivation that regulates the growth of intelligence is *intrinsic*. It is intrinsic because the development of intelligence is the result not of some outside factor but of an internal regulating force that is not solely or primarily dependent on the objects with which the intellect is in contact.

Here is the essence of the tragedy. Our schooling does not merely affect the intellect in an adverse manner by leaving it undernourished; more important, it fails to use the motivational forces that are present in any five- and six-year-old child. If we can ill afford to waste intellectual power, we can even less afford to neglect or push aside that constructive motivation which belongs to the child's personality.

7. In conclusion, the first job of our elementary schools today should be to strengthen the thinking foundation on which any particular learning is grounded. To do this administrators, teachers, and society at large must come to a fuller understanding of the natural development of the child's mind. Moreover, if early schooling aims to emphasize and purposefully nourish the thinking capacity of the child, it cannot look to performance in reading and writing as an immediate criterion of success. But in the long run, some positive transfer can reasonably be expected from a child who has been encouraged to develop intellectually for three or four years and who has been given a clear message that thinking is among the primary purposes of school life. Such a child will soon reach the point when further applications of his thinking skills require the content, variety, and articulation only reading can supply. In other words, he will spontaneously come to realize the value of reading and will learn to read in the easy, self-taught fashion of many preschool youngsters from homes where reading is an everyday activity.

These are the main points of the argument. The conclusion may not sound altogether convincing until you have a good grasp of what is meant by the thinking foundation on which learning is based. Our correspondence will therefore be focused almost exclusively on helping you to understand Piaget's theory of intellectual development and its application to grade school. However, to avoid misunderstandings, a few more observations on the relation of thinking and reading may be in order.

A nine-year-old girl from a suburban school spends two hours writing a few sentences about barometers. Her mind is occupied with copying and memorizing words, with descriptive knowledge about the appearance of these instruments. Very little, if any, thinking about the one aspect that could be challenging to her mind goes on

—that is, comprehension of the use or functioning of barometers. Thus, as far as her intellect is concerned, it is never challenged or fully exercised during these two hours. The time has been a loss for intellectual development—as not to grow is to diminish. Fortunately for the girl, she gets plenty of encouragement for intellectual growth at home, among her friends, and in other activities of her daily life, so that this "wasted" opportunity is perhaps not so serious.

But what about the less fortunate five- or six-year-old child who has neither a favorable past environment nor an encouraging present environment? Not to challenge his intelligence in school is truly a disaster, for the child is not intellectually awakened to an adequate degree outside school. With children at the threshold of operational intelligence, our schools are throwing away the last chance of plugging in where the natural strength of any human child lies. And they do this for the sake of imparting a specialized skill which in the early grade levels has very little to do with thinking. While the child is anxious to grow intellectually, society decrees that reading is going to be the criterion of scholastic success. The results of this psychological misunderstanding are seen in the thousands and tens of thousands of scholastic failures in school systems across the country.

Reading as such is not an intellectually difficult skill. A mental age of four years is ample as far as IQ is concerned—witness the success of early reading methods with some three- and four-year-old children. On the other hand, a mental age of eight or nine is certainly not too late for starting to read. My whole contention is that early reading does not have an intrinsic relation to intelligence and that its one-sided emphasis implies an underemphasis of intellectual development.

Let me say at the outset that I am not against reading, particularly if learning to read takes place in a setting that puts no undue stress on the child. I would quite be willing to match the reading skill of youngsters who spend the first four years in a "thinking" school with any products of the "reading" schools. Actually, this kind of comparison would merely be a statistical minimum and would be useless for practical purposes. If reading-focused programs could produce satisfactory results, we would not be forced to question them.

Indisputably, what we need is something better, something radically different. I am all for reading. I could not communicate with you so readily if it were not for the written word. Some of the best things in our culture and society would be—literally—unthinkable without it. If I appear to place thinking on a pedestal, I do so not in order to dethrone reading but in order to provide the base on which reading and specific learning can rest. Thus I am proposing that an early focus on thinking is better preparation for later emphasis on constructive learning through intelligent reading than the present emphasis on early reading.

These points contain about all I wish to say as a start. Let me know where further clarification is most urgent. This will help me to explain my thoughts about early education in a systematic manner without unduly taxing your patience.

Sincerely yours,

Piaget
on
thinking

PART ONE

Piaget's perspective

LETTER 2

Dear Teacher:

You are right in suggesting that the place to start further explanations of points in Letter 1 is with the concept of thinking or intelligence. I am not surprised at your observation that I have used the concept of intelligence in a different sense from that to which you are generally accustomed. Whereas you learned that different individuals within a given age group have different intelligence (i.e., IQ scores), and that by and large a child's intelligence, as measured by these scores, does not change as he gets older, I have continually referred to the growing intelligence or to the developing capacity to think. All along I have not seemed to put much emphasis on IQ scores as such.

Before I attempt to discuss these issues, let me ask you the same two questions I have directed to other teachers of the early grades. If somebody asked you whether one of the primary aims of elementary education—indeed, of all education —is to develop the child's capacity for thinking, without a moment's hesitation you would answer yes. Who could not be in favor of thinking? This is like asking whether you favor motherhood or mental health. Now I ask you the second question: "Can you tell me about situations during the ordinary school day in which you have challenged the children's thinking?"

11

A long pause follows. This kind of question has obviously not been asked before. What would you reply? Well, you are pointing to number skills. All right, if we take the mechanical, rote aspect out of early mathematics and there is still knowledge left. Anything else? Again a long pause.

Is it a fair question? I think so. If schools aim at making people think, why should it be unfair to ask how they go about it?

Some teachers will reply that the elementary grades, in the main, are less for thinking than for a preparation for thinking; that these grades are preparing the ground by teaching elementary skills of reading, writing, numbers, social habits, and other skills related to learning. I will not pursue other teachers' comments further, except to point out that in the final analysis my two questions lead logically to your original question: What is thinking?

Most teachers seem to grasp quite well the general sense of my questions. In particular, they seem to comprehend phrases like *capacity for thinking* or *to challenge children's thinking.* I am now suggesting that it is not sufficient for teachers to understand these phrases in a general fashion. As teachers, we should be able to have a very clear conception of what thinking is. How else will we know whether a certain activity challenges thinking or is a good preparation for it? As soon as we turn to defining general intelligence or thinking, we must avoid simplistic solutions and realize that we are asking for more than a ready verbal definition. The realm of thinking, including such concepts as knowledge and intellect, has been the object of endless speculations and philosophical viewpoints. While such philosophies may now seem old-fashioned and even devoid of relevant meaning, at the least thinking is not a quick and easy object for our comprehension.

Two common solutions to the problem reflect either an inappropriate subjectivism or an equally inappropriate objectivism. First, the subjectivist would say that thinking is any activity on the part of the individual that is hidden from an observer but is available to the introspective experience of the person. This answer is couched in terms of an introspective glance at the subjective process of thinking. This method has been a favorite of people in the past and present, wise men and common men, but it has led to no conceivable agreement akin to the agreement we enjoy concerning objects we can really glance at. In other words, the idea that we can look at thinking as we look at a table or a river is an illusion. If we could, we would long ago have agreed on what we see.

The second temptation is to make of the objective IQ score more than it was meant to be and propose that a technical definition ("operational definition") of intelligence is by itself an explanation of it. An operational definition of terms is entirely neutral; it is not explanatory. It can help or hinder depending on the state of the science. For example, defining air and fire as discrete, individual "elements" did much to delay progress in chemistry by obscuring the search for the real elements. A meaningful definition belongs at the end of an investigation, the final product of a painstaking inquiry; at the beginning, an explanatory definition can often thwart the effort and lead the investigator astray.

Enough has been said by laymen and professionals alike about the objective IQ score. It is clear that an IQ score is not and cannot be more than a statistically meaningful measure of certain standardized performances directly validated against scholastic success and therefore predictive of it. It is as readily affected by such factors as familiarity, motivation, personal experience, health, physical and social environment, and cooperation, as the acquisition of know-how in automechanics or skill in thrifty shopping and budgeting.

I am poor in both these skills, and I would be justifiably concerned if my performances were used to mark me as an incapable and unintelligent person. A similar concern motivates responsible people when they point to widespread misuses of intelligence-test scores. Using IQ-test performance to infer a low intellectual capacity in people who have a different culture is only one rather blatant example of such misuse. Apart from this, there are and will be untold individual cases of misuse of test scores if they are regarded as "really" measuring general intellectual capacity.

Standardized tests of intelligence have a certain predictive value when considered with a dozen other factors, some more and some less known, that may have as much or more predictive value for school achievement. For instance, at age five or six, it is reported, occupation and educational level of parents have a higher correlation with final school achievement than does measured IQ. Other important variables for which adequate measures are not available are motivational factors like need for scholastic achievement and social and emotional adjustment.

A major weakness in the "IQ approach" to intelligence is the acceptance of predetermined limitations on what a child can accomplish. This acceptance by teachers, counselors, and parents, and sometimes by the child himself, tends to encourage a passive attitude and to establish premature and unfounded standards of expectation. This tendency is as unfair to the gifted child as to the average or below-average scorer. As I suggested in Letter 1, in connection with reading, we teachers are too quick to attribute scholastic failures to measured IQ points. In reality no organic connection exists between reading performance and IQ once the four-year stage of intellectual development has been passed. In other words, it is not IQ but motivation that really counts in the business of learning to read.

I imagine that you can guess what stance I am taking on the relation of intelligence tests and capacity for thinking—in other words, on the relation of IQ score and the real McCoy. I would not say that they are unrelated—there are few measurable skills that are not positively related to IQ—but I certainly do object to any attempt to equate the two, as if the actual performance reflected in a score or a pattern of scores was, without further ado, a valid indicator of the child's general intelligence. I am even more strongly opposed to the extreme "objectivist" position, which externalizes intelligence and proposes that intelligence *is* what IQ tests measure.

If, in investigating human capacity for thinking, we reject the twin fallacies of introspective evidence and of a misplaced explanatory operationalism, we may find a viable alternative in the road Jean Piaget has taken. He framed the question thus: Generally, to comprehend something means to know how it comes about and what it leads to. Rather than asking for a definition of intelligence—what is the nature or essence of intelligence?—Piaget asked how the mature capacity for thinking comes about. He inquired into the history of intelligence, which history implies both an evolutionary and a developmental perspective. As a biologist, he observed the adaptation of species to various types of natural environment. And then, as a developmental psychologist, he observed another example of adaptation, namely, the spontaneous growth of thinking in the infant and child.

When we survey the vast variety of living organisms, we observe at all levels the presence of regulatory principles internal to the organism. You may be familiar with the principle of homeostasis. The physiological environment of an organism is kept within a narrow range of variation, a range conducive to the efficient functioning of the organism. Consider the function of green, leafy plants which ensures a delicate balance of oxygen input and output and provides an atmospheric condition suitable for living organisms. You can also include here instinctual behavior patterns of species of animals which maintain a healthy balance of food and living space. These kinds of regulation are found at all levels of life. They are internal to the living organism and serve two principal functions: to maintain the organism intact and to regulate the interactions of the organism with environmental events.

An organism exists only insofar as it *functions.* Biologists refer to adaptive functioning, which proceeds according to internal regulatory principles. Adaptive functioning manifests the regulatory principles and at the same time the structure of the organism. Each organism has a *structure*. Keep in mind that a structure is not the same as the particular organism under observation. An organism's structure can be said to be the totality of the organizational subsystems by which an organism belongs to a certain species (e.g., dog, human) and has specific functional capacities.

Perhaps I can illustrate the concepts of structure and functioning by means of an analogy taken from the workings of a nonbiological system familiar to all of us. Can anyone explain the functioning of a radio set without referring to the organization of the various parts that make up the set? There is no single thing to which you can point your finger and assert that this thing "explains" the radio. If we insist that one factor can explain a radio's functioning, we must resort to the factor of organization. The organization itself cannot be observed. It is inferred from the functioning of the radio. Moreover, the organization of the total radio set includes a great number of subsets, and each of these parts is again an organization relative to subparts, and so on.

Clearly, the proper functioning of a radio and the organization of a radio are just two sides of the same coin. In this sense, organization does not really "explain" functioning; it merely stresses a perspective that cannot be avoided when we try to come to an understanding of a radio set.

Now let us notice characteristic differences between a physical and a biological organization. The latter is a living organization—an organism. Consequently, functioning is not something that can be turned on and off like a radio. A living structure *is* a functioning structure. And whereas the organization of a radio is not modified through functioning, a living structure is affected by its functioning in a given environment. This interaction with the environment is not merely an imposition from outside, something added to a given structure. A biological structure stands in active relation to the environment. And this relation is knowledge.

Thus, the existence of a biological structure always implies that the organism has some knowledge of the environment. Knowing is here understood in a very broad sense and is much more inclusive than "intellectual" knowledge. It can be taken as synonymous with having information relevant to its functioning. An organism shows, by its functioning, adaptive knowledge. For instance, a dog who finds his way home manifests an internal structure of spatial orientation and localization which makes it possible for him to find his home in this and similar situations. We can say that the dog has some information about his environment, that he knows his way around the neighborhood. We realize, of course, that this is knowing entirely geared to external actions. The only way in which a dog can manifest this knowledge of localization is to move around in a meaningful manner. Even though this knowledge is active only in external actions and can therefore be called a "practical" knowledge, it is not correct to identify the *general* knowledge with any number of *particular* acts. Knowledge at all levels has a generalizable aspect which goes beyond given particular actions.

Piaget postulates that all psychological functioning has a structural aspect—it relates to underlying structures—and that in this way it deals with knowledge. It also has a dynamic aspect that relates to underlying energizing forces. This second aspect has not been directly investigated by Piaget. When we think of the forces of human life with its motivations, conscious and unconscious, its affects, emotions, values, and interests, the name of another biologist comes to mind. Freud was the great revolutionary who discovered causal connections and meaningful continuities where others merely observed disparate events and meaningless activities.

You recall that functioning is generally observable. It relates the internal structure to the external environment. In the case of the dog who is running home, we observe this functioning—that is, the way in which the dog reacts to successive spatial cues—and we can infer the dog's structured knowledge. We can look at this functioning and the underlying structure in two directions. Insofar as the functioning takes in or uses external cues in accordance with the internal structure, this process is called *assimilation*. Insofar as the functioning takes account of the particular and constantly changing newness of external situations—no two real situations are ever exactly alike—the organism *accommodates* its structure to particular aspects of the known situation. The fact that the dog can find his way home at an appropriate time (e.g., when whistled for or when hungry) from a large number of starting places and under a wide variety of conditions (light or dark, dry or wet) indicates *assimilation* of variable specific conditions to the general competency (scheme) of "knowing the way home." Conversely, to perceive accurately and to react appropriately to the myriad of changing cues and new cues is *accommodation,* in which the scheme of "going home" is constantly modified, enriched, and perhaps permanently altered by new experiences in an adaptive fashion. Assimilation therefore emphasizes the direction from the particular situation to the general structure; accommodation stresses the direction from the general structure to the particular situation. By the same token, assimilation focuses on what is essential to all knowing, namely, the sameness, communality, and generalization in a given situation; whereas accommodation focuses on what is particular, new, and different, and by doing so it provides the basis for change and learning.

A structure is always a totality of interrelated substructures, and Piaget calls *schemes* those substructures that underlie specific types of functioning. We could say that for Piaget interior schemes and knowledge are identical, if we take knowledge in the limited sense of generalizable information and abstract from the peculiar and dynamic aspects of the concrete situation in which an organism manifests knowledge.

I hear you ask a question: If knowledge is the same as an interior structure or scheme, what help is there in substituting one word for another? At this point I would answer this. Calling knowledge a "scheme" obviously does not "explain" knowledge, and is not meant to. It does provide a biological-psychological perspective in which one can analyze "knowledge" in a fruitful fashion. As the history of any science shows, new observations or technical gadgets are not so important to scientific development as the overcoming of established perspectives that led nowhere and the emergence of new perspectives that put the same old facts in a new light. We, in fact, have already given our analysis a new perspective by proposing that the functioning of a scheme can be viewed as two complementary processes, assimilation and accommodation. We have identified knowledge as the behavioral manifestation of structures within the organism. We have, moreover, suggested that internal principles regulate the relation between structures and functioning.

We will now analyze these regulatory principles further and, with Piaget, observe three broad kinds of regulations that can be inferred from psychological functioning. These are the rhythmic, reflex-like regulations of *instinctual* structures, the action-oriented regulations of *sensorimotor* structures, and the "intelligent" regulations of *operational* structures. Here, briefly, you have three levels of knowing as they become evident in the evolution of living organisms in general, and in the development of the individual human organism in particular.

Only the human species has the capacity for fully established operational regulations. Bear in mind, however, that reflex and sensorimotor regulations are still part and parcel of all human knowledge. Further, there are no hard and fast dividing lines between any two developmental levels. Concepts of stages should not suggest the existence of static developmental levels that are neatly separated; nor are such concepts meant to convey the idea of sudden jumps from one stage to the next. Piaget's concepts of stages in human development take the reflex regulations for granted and start with the sensorimotor stage; this is followed by the preoperational stage, which prepares for the concrete operational stage and leads to the final stage, the formal operational one. What is important is not, as is frequently implied, the notion of stage-related mental age (Piaget's stage norms cannot be treated like standardized IQ norms) but the regular sequence of stage-specific development.

However, it is high time that I stop and give you a chance to assimilate this novel perspective on thinking. Five main points were discussed:

1. Internal structures or schemes underly all organic functioning.
2. Structures imply self-regulatory principles that regulate the organism's functioning.
3. Functioning runs in two directions: assimilation of the environment to general schemes (knowledge), and accommodation of the schemes to the particulars of the environmental situation.
4. Knowing is identified with the schemes and the organizational, structural aspects of functioning.
5. Adult human intelligence is the most developed stage of operational regulations that derive from earlier action-oriented sen-

sorimotor and ultimately instinctual regulations.

Because I have spoken mainly of knowledge in general, let me finally suggest where thinking and intelligence fit into the picture. Piaget in one of his recent books, *Biology and Knowledge,* states that intelligence is simply (note what is simple for Piaget) the totality of available structures within a given organism at a given period of its development. This statement is contained in a footnote, of all things (on p. 357)! You can see that giving such a "definition" at the beginning of our inquiry would have been totally useless, and I don't want you to feel unhappy if you don't quite grasp Piaget's meaning after this first exposure to his perspective.

Piaget would have no objection if we referred to a type of instinctual intelligence that is built into the physiological system, or a practical intelligence tied to external actions. However, operational intelligence alone would be synonymous with what is ordinarily called human intelligence. Similarly, we do not ascribe thinking to instinctual or sensorimotor functioning; on the contrary, we commonly contrast these acts to thinking. This leaves operational intelligence as the characteristic structure that underlies intelligent thinking. To clarify our words, we will use the term "intelligence" to mean operational intelligence and "thinking" to mean the active functioning of operational intelligence. "Knowledge," on the other hand, is a suitable word for the structures and their functioning at all levels. However, in order to point out that knowledge has no existence apart from the knowing organism, we will as a rule avoid the word "knowledge" and in its place use "knowing."

Before we continue in Letter 3, I am anxious to get your reactions to this first encounter with Piaget's thinking.

Sincerely yours,

operational versus sensorimotor functioning

LETTER 3

Dear Teacher:

You suggest that Piaget's investigations may be taking a decidedly philosophical twist. Your reaction is quite natural for one who has been exposed only to limited aspects of psychology. If you mean by "philosophical" that the investigation of knowledge and its status in the objective world has traditionally been the province of philosophers, you are right. But philosophical inquiry is really more a matter of method than of content.

There was a time when philosophical inquiry into the status of the universe was claimed by philosophy and called cosmology. Typical of such inquiry was its unlimited scope; it tried to encompass in one grand view a totality of questions belonging to a variety of concerns and levels. Consider, for example, the various levels at which you may pose questions to a child: "Why is the third-quarter moon visible only after midnight?" "Why do we stand when the national anthemn is sung?" "Why should children start to save money when they are young?" It should help you as a teacher to recognize that all these questions admit reasonable answers, but that only the first is based *primarily* on a logical application of thinking structures. The first question is amenable to a certain kind of logical investigation, whereas the second and third must be investigated partly

20

in terms of social or personal values. These latter values belong to a level of contact with the world which quite properly goes beyond, but never against, logical thinking and includes factors of personal experience and commitment.

Admittedly, Piaget is concerned with some issues that have interested philosophers. He handles these issues, however, in a critical spirit of scientific inquiry and therefore opens the way to sceintific debate and possible agreement in matters that have traditionally been considered exclusively philosophical.

A brief diversion into Piaget's intellectual origins may shed some light on his theory and its applications for teachers. His early interest was in biology. When he was still in high school, he was offered the directorship of a museum on the strength of a paper he had published. Then he turned his attention to the theoretical foundations on which current biological knowledge rests. Later, he broadened his inquiry to include the general human capacity for the scientific enterprise. He planned to spend only a few years in this activity. Fortunately for us, his scientific curiosity and honesty compelled him to undertake the work of a child psychologist. Although this decision was made in the 1920s, Piaget continues to work today at many of the same tasks, demonstrating through systematic and controlled experiments how aspects of human knowing evolve.

⌈Piaget asked whether that capacity which makes scientific knowledge possible is the same as that capacity which underlies human intelligence in general. He thought so. To him it seemed that the basic skills underlying formal science — ordering, classifying, inferring, thinking in propositions and hypotheses (if . . . then . . .)—are the same as those skills which make spontaneous knowledge mature, stable, logically coherent, and open to new discoveries.⌉The genius of Piaget lies in his search for the developmental antecedents of scientific thinking rather than in any attempt at explanatory analysis of the finished product. As a result of his method, he has arrived at an explanation of intelligence that is not arbitrary, but is built into its own history.⌊In Piaget's own terse sentence: "The logic of development is the development of logic." That is, by observing objectively the regulations inherent in the development of intelligence, we can come to grips with the elusive phenomenon of the subjective, conscious intelligence and the logical functioning of that intelligence.⌋

In later correspondence I hope to be able to translate Piaget's theoretical concepts into classroom activities. In the meantime think about what it means to understand—for example, to understand a radio. It means that you comprehend to some degree how it functions and how it is constructed. Turning to another type of knowing, what does it mean to understand a Schubert trio? Obviously, one need not, as player or listener, compose the musical structure, but in a sense one does reconstruct the original composition, and thereby one knows or comprehends the musical meaning of the trio. The analogy between the construction of a musical composition and of human intelligence is enlightening for additional reasons.

You would not refer to a Schubert trio as "true" in the same way that 4 + 7 equals (and cannot but equal) eleven. There is a "required-ness" or necessity in mathematical or logical knowing that simply does not exist for other mental constructions. Even at the sensorimo-tor level, many situations have a certain obvious "practical" neces-sity; for instance, the only way to walk is to move one's legs, and the only way to get a cup of coffee is to reach out for it. Musical construc-tions, unlike logical constructions, do not have this logical necessity; yet, for all that, they are not whimsical products of an idiosyncratic fancy. History, if not contemporary criticism, separates the truly beautiful from lesser imitations, and eventually we recognize an ob-jectivity even in things that cannot be put into logical rules.

The development of intelligence shares two interesting points in common with musical knowing. First, no person can claim (as many would like to claim for intelligence) that a musical composition is a copy of reality. Quite obviously, nobody could identify the original that has been copied, for example, by a Haydn symphony or a Brahms quintet. Second, no person would assert (as many would like to as-sert for intelligence) that the rules of music are imposed from the outside world or are present at birth. Although intelligence in its final, mature state consists, in fact, of stable logical rules, everybody can observe for himself that a baby is not born equipped with these rules. Only a great number of years after the attainment of language and some manner of conscious reflection do these rules become stable and take on the characteristic of logical necessity. Hence, as with music, Piaget proposes that knowing is never just a passive copy of reality; it is a constructing on the part of the human subject that tends toward some measure of objectivity. Unlike music or other creative activities, the subjective constructing of logical intelligence does lead to a stable and consistent system of rules. These rules impose themselves on the knowing subject, not as norms dictated from outside but as belonging to the objective aspect of the human subject. They express that objective aspect in an explicit form on which the adult person can reflect.

We should not assume, therefore, at the beginning of our inquiry on intelligence, that whenever the word "subjective" is used we are in the realm of the unpredictable, the fanciful, the unscientific. Some such fears are at the bottom of behaviorists' almost neurotic avoidance of words that smack of anything mental or conscious. After all, intelligence deals with a mental process on which we can consciously reflect, and wishing these mental factors away does not change the phenomenon that science must study. But in Piaget's perspective, subjectivity need no longer be considered the opposite of objectivity. The adult's reflective experience of subjectivity can now be seen as the developmental end-result of a more primitive functioning that has no concomitant subjective consciousness. Finally, thinking and acting need not be conceptualized as two separate activities; rather, thinking should be taken as synonymous with "intelligent" action.

Where should one look for the antecedents of mature intelligence? Piaget based his answers on detailed, systematic observations of his own three children. Obviously, at the level of infancy there could be no question of a theoretical intelligence for at this level we are dealing only with sensorimotor intelligence. It became immediately apparent that the infant is not endowed by nature with even the simplest sensory or motor skills. At birth, for instance, he can perform no directed, purposeful motor activity or well-focused sensory activity.

The infant carries within him, however, the capacity to develop by acting on the environment. He does this gradually, consistently, and inexorably, regardless of the specifics of the environment. I am not suggesting the absurdity that an infant can develop in a vacuum or in an isolation chamber that would just keep him physically alive. When I say "environment," I imply not only the constantly changing physical world but also a biologically adaptive human environment, which at all times and in all places includes one's own body and the bodies of other human beings. Beneath the changing appearances is an invariability or sameness against which the changes and movements stand out. Thus, there are always some things that move and others that appear stationary, some things that can be touched and others that are out of immediate reach, some things that appease the appetite when put into one's mouth, others that don't, and so on.

This is the environment into which human babies are born and through which and in which they attain general structures of functioning that we eventually recognize as intelligence. Any mother or father who observes the growing infant can list some of the attainments common to all babies.

A ten-month-old baby happens to glance at a briefcase in the far corner of the room. He fixes his eyes on the object. He begins to orient his whole body toward it. One can almost feel that he already grasps the briefcase. But he is still far from it, and rather awkwardly he begins to crawl toward it. A table stands in the middle of the room between the baby and the briefcase. The baby passes one chair successfully and then finds himself close to a leg of the table. Now he no longer sees the briefcase. As he lifts his head to continue his travels, he almost touches with his face and arm the table cloth that is hanging from the table. The edge of the cloth moves a little. The baby is now quite fascinated by this hanging, movable stuff. His attention, until that moment riveted on the briefcase, is now all focused on the table cloth. The baby leans to his right and, lifting up his left arm, moves the cloth again and again. The baby's reaction to the cloth could be described as a repeated grasping and letting go with a rhythmic, circular movement of the left hand.

The actions we observed were the product of many weeks' development. The child demonstrated a number of practical know-hows; the child—in Piaget's language—has developed certain sensorimotor schemes that were not present at birth. He was able to focus his senses and his body's orientation on things that struck his interest; moreover, he was able to coordinate these skills to a considerable degree. He could look at something and at the same time handle it. He could visually observe something and move his body in a coordinated fashion in the direction of the observed object. He could notice a causal connection between the movement of his hand and the movement of an external thing, and he could repeat this event in a quasi-purposeful manner.

However, some things this baby was not able to do. First and foremost, his attention to things was completely action-dependent. It was initially aroused by some accidental action: the baby happened to glance at the briefcase, or he happened to touch the table cloth. However, the attention, and with it the attended thing, disappeared as soon as something new got in the way and distracted the baby from the goal of his original activity.

A few months later this baby's functioning will appear much more stable in that it will show greater attention and goal-directedness, but it will still be an action-oriented and action-dependent functioning. For instance, the older infant is no longer as easily distracted by new events and continues his search or movements toward a desired thing even though the goal of his activity is temporarily outside his field of vision. In addition, he can initiate some interesting event, like pulling on a string and setting a window shade in motion; he is not merely at the mercy of accidentally produced events. Moreover, he can recognize the desired milk bottle even if it is handed to him upside down. Instead of helplessly screaming, not knowing what to do with this unfamiliar object, he can turn the bottle around and enjoy it, as if he knew quite well how to coordinate the different spatial aspects of the bottle.

In Piaget's terminology, the child has developed more coordinated and more stable structures than before. He has now definitely acquired the scheme of means-end relation; that is, he can perform an action in order to obtain a goal not immediately obtainable. Likewise, he has better coordinated schemes toward things in the environment and, in general, a better coordination in spatial orientation. Such a child exhibits what Piaget calls "action-intelligence," which is comparable in many ways to the functioning of subhuman animals.

At this developmental level we need not hesitate to use the word "knowledge." Of course, an infant past his first birthday knows his mother, knows his own body as different from others, knows his playthings, his crib, his room, and the layout of his home. How does he "know" these things? He knows them by adaptive, coordinated external action toward them, not by any theoretical, reflective knowing. The infant does not—as we can do—separate thinking from external action; he "thinks" *in external action.* The infant's logic is thus an action logic, just as the infant's intelligence is a practical, sensorimotor intelligence.

Notice the logic of this infant. He has many "concepts," if among concepts we include practical recognitions and functional reactions to things. He makes "judgments," if by judgment we refer to the infant's assimilation of singular, concrete instances into general schemes. He makes progress and "learns" by functioning better, insofar as he constantly accommodates an identical scheme to particular features of singular instances. Most important, the child's intelligence makes "abstractions," if we take the word "abstract" in a simple, relative sense. By this I mean that in the development of knowing, a later behavioral structure is always abstracted from an earlier, more primitive behavioral structure.

We can observe, for instance, that the scheme of hand-eye coordination derives from the two earlier schemes of grasping and visual focusing. These early schemes function separately, if not at cross purposes. A four-month-old baby may feel some object in his hand without being able to bring it into visual focus, and he may see a thing which he can bring into his hand only by accident or not at all. Gradually these two sensorimotor schemes are mutually assimilated, and the new scheme of hand-eye coordination develops. It becomes manifest in the child's ability to focus his eyes on things that are in his hand or to handle, if they are within reach, things that look interesting. The process of development from the earlier actions to the later scheme can be called an abstraction, since the scheme derives from the generalizable aspects of these actions. We may call the generalizable aspect of any activity its *form* and the particular aspects its *content*. In our example of hand-eye coordination, the content of the earlier schemes would be the various particular things the baby sees or handles. The developing scheme of hand-eye coordination "abstracts" from the content of the earlier schemes and coordinates the forms of these separate activities. Piaget emphasizes how important it is to realize that we are dealing here with a kind of abstraction that is directed at the form of the activities. The form or the coordination of the human action is not something in the environment, it is the structuring of the action and does not exist apart from the action.

I have sketched here Piaget's concept of *formal abstraction*. This concept is vital to his theory. It suffices for the moment if it provides you with a tentative answer to the question: "Where do new schemes come from?" The answer is: "From the differentiation and coordination of earlier schemes by means of formal abstraction."

Now that we have described some characteristic features of sensorimotor intelligence, you may ask how the child develops further toward adult intelligence. To explain this I must introduce a new concept. This is the concept of *object formation* and the resulting *scheme of the permanent object*.

For the sensorimotor organism, objects as such do not exist. Such a statement sounds almost heretical to those readers, who are used to taking for granted that the objective reality of things is the one basic starting point of all knowing. Yet, at least in the sensorimotor period, solid evidence indicates that for the organism things do not exist apart from the actions of the organism on them. We have seen this dramatically in the case of the young infant who lost interest in the briefcase—"out of sight, out of mind." In the somewhat older infant, we have described more advanced actions that do not go beyond action-knowing. Certainly the older infant knows his way around the home, but this practical knowing cannot be manifested apart from the action of external locomotion.

Object formation, which occurs at about age 1½, means the acquisition of the scheme of the permanent object. It implies that things in the physical world are taking on a degree of stability and permanency which they did not possess in the child's earlier contacts with the world. As far as the growing child is concerned, the world is beginning to extend beyond the spatial and temporal immediacy of external activity.

Observe a two-year-old who is beginning to show his capacity to dissociate his personal action from his knowing of objects. If you hide a toy which he finds pleasant and attractive, he will systematically look for it. An observer of the child's behavior can conclude that this child knows about the existence of objects and about the unlikelihood that they disappear into nothingness. Even when the child's attention is drawn away from it, he will persist in going after the toy. If it is hidden under one of three boxes and the child does not find it in the first, he will immediately look for it in another and continue until he finds the thing, as if he knows that a permanent thing must be found by a systematic search.

Comparing the search activity of this child with the sensorimotor search of a younger infant, you will notice that sensorimotor activity, insofar as it implies knowing, manifests a knowledge in which one cannot separate the knowing organism from the particular object that is known. The infant knows by doing. But now, for the first time, a new kind of knowing appears, a knowing that cannot be entirely tied to a particular object, a knowing that abstracts from particular features.

In the acquisition of the scheme of the permanent object, we observe for the first time an abstraction with a degree of generality that is not tied to the person's own activity. Thanks to this "formal" abstracting the child can "think" of the existence of an object without externally reacting to it. For the moment this seems a small enough accomplishment; it is still many years from the theoretical knowledge that we associate with the abstract thinking of verbal propositions. But it is a significant beginning, and it marks the threshold where practical intelligence turns into theoretical intelligence; it marks the beginning of thinking. Object-formation in the sense of incipient objective knowing is the first characteristic of the transition beyond the sensorimotor stage and illustrates one of the hallmarks of mature thinking.

A second characteristic, symbol formation, follows from object formation so as to become equally important Symbol behavior cannot occur at the sensorimotor stage, for practical knowing of an event is consistently tied to a personal action toward the event. The organism externalizes its knowing. The external act does not *represent* knowing but *is* the knowing. In order to symbolize knowing, the organism must free knowing, at least in part, from its ties to external action. This dissociation of knowing is first demonstrated in object formation.

Naturally, a sensorimotor organism can respond to signals and orient its functioning according to perceptual cues. An animal running down a hill takes account of innumerable features of the surface and directs his running accordingly. Animals also give signals and communicate with each other, and they can be trained to react in a specific manner to certain signals. But all these signals or conditioned stimuli are consistently tied to the appropriate external action. In signal behavior the organism does not differentiate the signal from the action. In this sense, the signal is an undifferentiated sign.

Symbol behavior requires the active use of a special sign, namely, a differentiated sign or symbol. A signal is an event to which the sensorimotor infant reacts more or less in the same way in which he reacts to the "real" thing. But a symbol, as a differentiated sign, is like something known to which the child responds in a variety of ways according to his level and situation of knowing. A symbol represents knowing, and the child knows it as such. When a three-year-old child plays "mother" or "going to bed," the child's gestures could not take place if the child's knowing of mother or sleeping were tied to physical actions. Sensorimotor knowing of sleeping, you will recall, is *actual* sleeping. When the child plays sleeping we can conclude that his knowing is beyond the sensorimotor stage, that it is no longer entirely tied to the external action, and that therefore the child is capable of representing his knowing in *symbolic* sleeping.

In summary, then, sensorimotor knowing is practical behavior—

manifest in and wed to external actions. The transition to a different stage of knowing is characterized by the child's capacity to recognize the independent existence of physical objects apart from his own personal actions on them. This resulting knowing is the scheme of the permanent object. It is the first invariant (constant) which the developing intelligence constructs by way of formal abstractions from the general coordinations of sensorimotor acts. It is the first glimmer of "theoretical" behavior, so to speak. As a consequence of this partial dissociation of thinking from personal action, the child is now capable of representing his thinking in symbolic behavior.

Further progress of the developing intelligence, which I will discuss in my next letter, consists in the construction of increasingly more stable invariants. They will form the solid framework on which intelligent behavior and mature reasoning rest. Symbol formation poses a special challenge to the growing intelligence. We shall learn to look on symbols as an indispensable support to thinking and at the same time as an obstacle to be overcome. In fact, growth of the capacity to think goes hand in hand with increased independence of thinking from personal symbols.

Before I close, I want to say something by way of encouragement. Piaget's theory is a whole. You cannot expect to understand each aspect in piecemeal fashion unless and until you understand the whole. On the other hand, by repeating similar theoretical points and viewing them from different angles you will find that later letters will clarify early letters and vice versa. Also, as Piaget reminds us Americans, who are always in a hurry and want to speed up development, assimilation is the only way in which communicated knowledge can become part of an organism, and assimilation takes time.

Best wishes until next time.

Yours sincerely,

concepts: verbal versus operational

LETTER 4

I like your remarks about "jumping in and swimming," and "letting yourself go." But you seem baffled by the questions Piaget raises, in particular those about the formation of the object scheme. As a teacher you know that questions frequently point up unanalyzed assumptions that are taken for granted. This, by the way, is why children's questions frequently reveal their underlying thinking more than their answers do.

We have been steeped in a certain attitude toward the nature of knowing. For us, objective facts exist from the start; human knowing implies a process by which these facts are made available to us. If, in our search for an understanding of human intelligence, we begin with the traditional perspective on knowing, we will ask such questions as "By what means does a person get hold of objective facts?"

Piaget, who has a different outlook, starts with the functioning organism in adaptive contact with the world. This functioning manifests the organism's internal organization. Instead of a stimulus to which a response has to be initially associated, there is the organic, internal scheme of the infant. The functioning of the scheme always implies the assimilation of particular content (primarily from the environment) and the accommodation of the scheme to

30

this content. Nowhere is there a stimulus apart from a response, and the question of how a "subjective" response becomes attached to an "objective" stimulus is not of primary interest.

This is what you mean by "letting yourself go." You can't keep asking of Piaget the same questions you were wont to pose within a stimulus-response-reward paradigm of learning.

You still sound somewhat confused about the way I use words like "scheme," "knowing," "intelligence," "thinking." Do I make separately existing entities out of these notions? Not at all. If I seem to (as when I speak of a developing intelligence or a knowing that is dissociated from external acts), this is purely a manner of speaking. The individual person alone has existence and functions; all else has a borrowed existence and is a conceptual aspect of the concretely existing and functioning individual. A person has a scheme or knowledge, a person has intelligence, a person does the thinking. I will even go further and say that none of these notions has any observable existence; none is a thing, not even an organ like the heart or the brain. Knowing, as the structuring aspect of life, is akin to living. I cannot point at knowing. It becomes manifest, as does life itself, in observable actions. Physiological structures and brain structures are of course prerequisite to psychological functioning. But the schemes of knowing are not identical with these. We are speaking here of structures on the level of an organism's psychological functioning, not of physiological functioning. Moreover, you point out that I use the words "intelligence" and "knowing" interchangeably. This is true, particularly when I refer to the general structures of knowing rather than the knowing of a particular fact.

Like other terms we will use, the English word "knowledge" is a difficult and ambiguous term, and we must here be constantly on guard against abdicating thinking in favor of semantic habits. If you take the following list of sentences literally, you can never make sense out of all these statements. (1) "A person has knowledge." Here knowledge is a possession like a shirt. (2) "Problem-solving is an act of knowledge." Here knowledge is a certain type of activity, in contrast to other acts belonging to other types (motivation, perception). (3) "Knowledge leads to successful behavior." Here knowledge is an internal prelude to a certain kind of external behavior. Another difficulty is that in the sentence, "A person knows something," the predicate may refer to a habitual knowledge or to a present activity (thinking) which actualizes this knowledge.

It will help if, within our context, you think of knowledge as the structuring, generalizable aspect of a person's functioning. It is always related to, and is one aspect of, any human activity. Hence, the use of the active form "knowing" is preferable, for it is less open to misinterpretation than the noun "knowledge." On the other hand, it is important to realize that no activity is utterly devoid of any knowing aspect. In short, knowing is an activity, but it is not to be thought of as distinct from other, nonknowing activities. Thinking refers to actual knowing in which an individual applies his operational intelligence to a particular content.

At the sensorimotor level, the very young infant has no occasion to separate knowing from action because knowing is consistently tied to the appropriate action. At the transition to the next stage of development, however, we have already encountered a scheme that is not entirely bound to external action, namely, the scheme of the permanent object, which ushers in the eventual separation of object and subject. Now we have to be on guard not to make independently existing entities of either the object or the subject. Knowing essentially remains what it was, an activity on the part of the organism in functional contact with the world. The apparent separation of the knowing organism (subject) and the known event (object) is only the result of our thinking activity. In reality, the known object at the operational level (the concept of bottle) is still identical with the knowing subject (the knowing of the bottle), just as at the sensorimotor level the known thing (e.g., bottle) is identical with the activity of the knowing organism (e.g., drinking).

This is what Piaget has in mind when he constantly stresses that operational knowing is an activity, even though it is not always manifest in external action. For my part, I have no hesitation in speaking of *knowing behavior* or *thinking behavior,* because for me behavior is not just any random motor activity, but an activity which manifests something about the organism's structure. To see the relation between the two developmental stages, remember that a functioning sensorimotor scheme is a sensorimotor action and that a functioning operational scheme is a thinking action.

In Piaget's terminology, "operation" is short for "operational scheme." But besides this structural use ("A person has an operation"), there is also a functional use ("A person does an operation; thinking is an operation"). This is potentially confusing. All I can do is remind you that structure and function are correlative terms and refer to two sides of the same coin.

Moreover, Piaget employs the word "operation" only *in the strict sense* and designates the transitional period between sensorimotor and operational as *preoperational.* The thinking of a three-year-old child Piaget calls preoperational in comparison with the strict operations of which a six- or seven-year-old child is capable. However, when we compare a three-year-old to the sensorimotor child, the most decisive break is the first dissociation which makes thinking possible. Even though the object scheme is still far from a perfect operation, it has already an operational character as distinct from sensorimotor functioning. For this reason we can call the transitional period "operational" when operational is used *in the wide sense.* Keep in mind that the schemes of the transitional period are not perfect operations but only tend toward them. In this stricter sense they are called "preoperational."

To give you a quick overview, here is an outline of Piaget's main developmental stages with approximate ages at which they first appear and some typical activities:

Stage	Onset	Typical activities
Sensorimotor	Birth	Perception, recognition, means-end coordination
Preoperational	1–2	Comprehension of functional relations, symbolic play
Concrete operational	6–7	Invariant structures of classes, relations, numbers
Formal operational	11–13	Propositional and hypothetical thinking

I would now like to continue our discussion of mental development and focus on the emergent preoperational activities that follow the establishment of the object scheme at the end of the sensorimotor period. You recall that the formation and use of symbols was seen as a consequence of the operational aspect of the child's knowing. The two-year-old child who knows something about his mother's activity shows off this knowing by playing mother. The same is true about being put to bed: he may repeat some external aspects of the going-to-bed activity in a gestural pantomime and thereby manifest his knowing. At this age, when the child begins to imitate external activities for the sake of symbolizing some knowing, he also begins to imitate the verbal language of society. The child, who during the sensorimotor stage communicated by means of direct actions or signals, readily adapts the newly acquired symbol skills to social communication.

You may have noticed that for Piaget "symbol" is a very broad term that covers any event (including verbal language) which represents something a person knows. Since we are no longer dealing merely with practical knowing, symbols are a necessary guide to evaluating the status of intellectual development. If you wanted to investigate a three-year-old child's comprehension of the social family structure, how would you go about it? Even if the linguistic competence of the child was excellent, you would hardly expect the child to come up with adequate verbal definitions. A better way would be to observe the symbolic activity of the child playing family.

The child finds it quite natural to use any arbitrary things to represent known things as long as there is some figural likeness that relates one to the other. If he plays family, he need not necessarily play with puppets that look like human beings. He may be quite content to play with sticks of varying lengths, so that there is a rough correspondence between length and age, the longer sticks representing older people, the shorter ones younger people, and the tiny ones infants and babies. In a like manner, a pencil can be a jet plane or it can stand for a river, a bed, or what not. A child's intellectual growth is, therefore, readily reflected in the way he uses symbols, including verbal language.

Some other aspects of the child's growing intelligence can be observed by outward behavior that uses symbols only minimally. For instance, line up three different objects on the edge of a round table. Put a four-year-old child on a chair with wheels on it. Move him in one direction along the table and let him observe the order in which the objects are lined up. After he can recall the order, blindfold him, move him to the other side of the table, and have him tell you which object he will encounter first, second, third. The child's *scheme of ordering* is probably not sufficiently developed so that he is able to reverse the order or so that he even expects the order to be reversed.

Another behavioral example that does not need any symbols at all is the sorting of a pile of blocks of different colors, sizes, and shapes. Take three hoops and put them in partly overlapping position; then start putting blue blocks in one, triangles in another, and small blocks in the third. Put those blocks that do not fit into one of the three classes outside the hoops. Have the four-year-old child watch you. Let him continue the sorting, and correct him if necessary. Observe where he puts a blue triangle, or a small blue circle. Does he know where to put small blue triangles? Here we are observing the child's *scheme of classification.* I want you to note that no overt symbolization of any kind is part of the procedure, and I can see no reason to theorize that the child must use symbolic means (e.g., verbal concepts) in order to classify. However, it is unlikely that a four-year-old's system of classification is sufficiently developed to master this rather complex task.

Finally, take a bag, and in front of a five-year-old child put ten yellow balls and one blue ball into the bag. Have him shake the bag and then guess which color he will draw. Let him take out one ball, and whatever the outcome, let him guess again. Will he consistently make the more reasonable prediction, will he alternate, or will he simply guess on no rational basis? In other words, does the child manifest in any way the operational *scheme of probability?* Success on this kind of a task is not usually seen before age eight.

I have given you these examples to impress upon you that in the study of intellectual development, even if we sometimes use verbal or other symbols as a convenient or necessary means of communication, our primary focus is on the operational schemes and not on the symbols in which they may be expressed. Schemes of relation, classification, spatial and temporal perspective or probability, these and similar structures are the stuff of which intelligence is made. They can be expressed in actions, in images, in gestures, in verbal language; the medium in which they are expressed does not alter the operational aspect of knowing. Consequently, we must train ourselves to look beyond the symbol to the knowing scheme which lies beneath it.

If we do this, it becomes at once apparent that intelligence, especially during the early ages, has a general aspect that pervades all kinds of activities. A child who has not yet developed a stable classificatory scheme is likely to manifest this conceptual failure in practically any aspect where class relations come into play. He cannot understand geographical notions of city, county, state, country; he cannot grasp relationships beyond the most immediate family; he cannot comprehend time concepts; he may find it hard to realize that a policeman can also be a father or that the same architectural structure can be called both "building" and "house."

You see here that we are dealing with general knowing. It would be quite unthinkable that a child should excel and have mature concepts in one of the stated areas and be immature in others. By this I do not imply that there are no variations in developmental maturity across different areas; but substantial classificatory skill in just one aspect of reality, with general weakness in all others, simply does not occur.

The most striking area in which young children appear to fail is in the use of verbal language, yet frequently we consider progress in use of language the hallmark of a growing intelligence. We will come back to this matter of language, since it looms so large in the mind of all educators. But is it not obvious that little children cannot but fail in symbolic expressions when they do not have the intellectual capacities on which the expressions rest?

Piaget once used the term "egocentric" to characterize the thinking of children before they reach the strictly operational stage, beginning around age seven. He now wishes that he had never used this expression because so many people misinterpreted it to mean selfish or constantly thinking about oneself. Piaget meant nothing of the sort. What he wanted to point out was that the thinking of preoperational children is centered on their own personal perspective, on their own personal experience, and that they find it difficult to overcome and transcend that personal experience.

This characteristic of egocentrism places the preoperational child midway between the sensorimotor and the strictly operational child. At the sensorimotor level thinking is not possible because knowing is entirely tied to personal, external actions; at the transitional stage thinking becomes possible since knowing is beginning to be dissociated from external actions, but personal actions still dominate thinking and give it a personal flavor. Only with the establishment of the first strict operations around age six do we encounter stable and objective thinking which can freely abstract from personal experience and therefore transcend it.

The schemes of the preoperational child, even though they can function apart from fully external actions, still depend on and function within personal experience. The word "horse" means something quite different to a three-year-old child from the country who lives in the company of horses than it does to a city child who has seen a horse only in picture books. The personal experience of each child may be reflected in the images evoked by the word "horse" and in the sentences in which the word is used. Each child's knowing of the concept of horse is largely a function of personal background. The operational structure of classification will make it possible to overcome the personal experience and regard the species horse in an objective fashion.

Perhaps a better example lies in the question of houses and buildings. I asked a nine-year-old child who lives in a suburb whether there were more buildings than houses, to which he answered that there were more houses. Asked why, he explained that "houses were in buildings." I looked skeptical and replied, "Don't you think that houses *are* buildings?" He said, "Yes, of course." There you have a beautiful instance of children's thinking. Apparently he first identified house with home (because his and his friend's homes are houses) and buildings with apartment buildings. Hence his remark that houses are in buildings—that is, homes are in apartment buildings. But he was not overconcerned about this relation of inclusion and on prodding admitted that houses were buildings. Do you get the flavor of this child's egocentric shifting? He first takes the verbal symbols according to his personal experience; yet he is vaguely aware of a more objective sense of the words without realizing that the two different meanings result in contradictory statements.

Wait now, and listen to how a child of the same age living in New York City reacted. To the question whether there were more buildings or houses he quickly replied, "Buildings." Asked why, he pointed out that there are many buildings but few houses. Obviously this child's personal experience, different from that of the surburban child, colored the meanings he attached to words.

If children's concepts at age nine (they are already in grade three!) are still so fluid and uncertain, you can imagine the thinking world of children at an earlier age. Piaget has recorded many apt illustrations of which we will mention a few. Take two sticks of equal length and place them horizontally in front of a four-year-old child. Ask him whether the sticks are equally long or whether one is longer than the other. The child will say that they are the same, and you can verify for yourself that he can differentiate between short and long by sorting sticks of two obviously unequal lengths. After the child has recognized equality of length, move one stick slightly to the right. Ask the same question as before and, for sure, the child will say that the stick you moved is now longer.

To return to an age which is of direct concern to you as an elementary-school teacher, ask a seven-year-old child to draw you a bottle half-filled with water. When he has done this, draw the bottle—without water—in a tilted position and ask him to add the water level. Or take a match, put it half over the edge of a table, and slightly tap the overhanging part. Let a nine-year-old child observe what happens. Give him a paper on which is drawn the table and the overhanging match with the head of the match marked in solid black. Tell him to draw the successive positions of the match as it flips over and finally falls on the floor. Look at the child's drawings of the water level or of the positions which a falling match is supposed to take. I do not see how any person can observe these kinds of behavior samples and still maintain that knowing is a passive copy of "objective" facts.

Why does length change for the young child with changing position? Because in the child's experience length is a relative term— "from here to there." When you move the *there* further away, the distance gets longer unless you compensate for it by also moving the *here.* But this little mental trick is not yet in the child's repertory. Similarly, young children cannot handle simultaneously two spatial coordinate systems. They draw the water level in relation to the tilted bottle and not to the horizontal ground. As for the falling match, this moves more like the child himself when he makes a belly flop into the water; the successive turning around an imaginary axis is simply not present to the child's mind.

Would you have any objection if I call the behavioral skills we have sampled so far by the name *concepts* and say that children have not yet adequately developed concepts of class inclusion (house-building), length, horizontality, rotation? Now I am using the word "concept" in a different sense from the one to which you are accustomed. The main difference is that for me a concept is primarily a behavioral structure in the form of an operational scheme or, as Piaget abbreviates it, an operation. Whether the concept is symbolized in gestures, in drawings, or in words, or is simply manifest in coordinated activity, is besides the point. When I refer to a child's having the concept of rotation, I mean that this child comprehends something about the physical phenomenon, that he can point it out by gestures or draw it. Never mind whether he knows or does not know the English word "rotation." The same holds for the other concepts. It is the behavior that counts, not the symbols. For Piaget concepts are in the realm of behavior—namely, thinking—and not in the realm of symbols.

The concepts we have stressed, together with other general concepts pertaining to time, space, quantity, probability, identity, combination, negation, number, relation, substitution, and so on, become serviceable and functional to the degree that they become increasingly more operational. This becoming more operational is the work of formal abstraction; it is manifest in the increased independence of the operations from personal experience. (Remember that formal abstraction focuses on what is general and common to all men in experience and, therefore, abstracts from what is personal and idiosyncratic in the experience.) One way in which progress in thinking is evident is the better (or, as we would say, more correct) use of verbal language. But there is similar evidence to support the statement that the use of any symbol system, drawing, pantomime, playing, and the like, improves with the growing intelligence.

Because of our customary preoccupation with verbal definitions we tend to take a static position toward concepts. Mention the teaching of concepts and our first reaction is a move toward the dictionary. As if concepts were in books! Concepts are schemes of action, not things to look at. Strange that here Piaget seems to be more a behaviorist than the most rigid learning theorist. A "real" concept (that is, one comprehended by somebody) is a person's use of an operational scheme with its implied assimilation and accomodation. A person "has" a concept when he assimilates a given situation to available general schemes, or, from another perspective, when he accomodates, that is, applies general schemes to particular situations.

Perhaps it may help if we look at the relation of concept and scheme from a different angle and consider that *an operational scheme is a concept.* When the operational scheme is not fully operational, it is in part dependent on personalized experience. The resulting concept is immature, egocentric, and labile. Piaget points out that personal experience is always unidirectional and *irreversible.* An actual step taken in a certain direction at a certain moment is a unique behavior that cannot be undone. Schemes become fully operational only when they are fully *reversible.* Reversibility of a scheme implies that the human subject has the possibility of making mental experiments: doing and undoing, going in one direction and compensating for it in another direction (e.g., length); regarding a thing as belonging to one class and at the same time to another class, and relating classes to each other (e.g., class inclusion); coordinating one perspective with another perspective (e.g., horizontality), or transforming successively the position of a thing moving around a fixed point (e.g., rotation).

These concepts cannot be directly registered from the environment. They are constructions on the part of the thinking subject. The greater the contribution of this subject, the greater the resulting objectivity. Concepts become objective and stable to the degree that they are anchored in the invariants which the subject constructs by means of formal abstractions.

When operational structures are fully achieved, beginning at ages 11 to 13, the human organism is subject to operational regulations that are far superior to sensorimotor regulations or to the "intuitive" regulations of the preoperational period. Sensorimotor regulations require trial and error. There just is no sure way of keeping a sensorimotor infant from touching the proverbial hot stove except the baby's experience, with its painful consequences. For the preoperational period Piaget used the word "intuitive" to denote "imagined," "self-experienced" situations from which the preoperational child draws functional rules of behavior. For instance, a three-year-old child knows that a container gets fuller the more you put into it; or that you cannot push through an opening a thing that is wider than the opening. (This latter knowing is by no means obvious, as anybody can observe when a toddler tries furiously to force something through the railing of a playpen, finally gives up after many fruitless attempts, and perhaps only then tries some other way.) At times the intuitive rules serve the child well; at other times they lead him astray. The intuitive rule, "The older, the bigger," is on the whole fine when applied to a population of children; but it is simply wrong to apply this rule to adults.

Strictly operational rules, in contrast, abstract from self-experienced situations and impose themselves as obvious and natural on our behavior. If a house is one kind of building, there *must* be more buildings than houses. These rules are experienced by reflection as necessary and universally true. It is instructive to consider the reaction of a five-year-old child who believes that there is more water in a slender beaker than in the wider beaker from which it was filled, even though he saw that initially there were two wide beakers containing the same amount of water. Two years later the same child may think it ridiculous even to entertain the notion that the quantity of water can change with the shape of the container. If it were merely a matter of copying reality, how is it that the seven-year-old child "registers" something as unquestionably true when a few months earlier he seriously held the opposite view?

But development is not a matter of cumulatively taking in outside information. The answer to the observed change of behavior is that during the period from five to seven years of age some of the child's schemes become fully operational. At five his judgment still relied in part on his own personal experience, according to which "higher means more." At seven too he may quite well have been surprised at the height of the water level in the slender beaker relative to the water level from which it was poured. But the scheme to which the situation was assimilated gave the child the skill to compensate for the perceptual surprise. He understood that what was gained in height was proportionally lost in width. This is what reversibility means; because of the available operational scheme the child could mentally reverse the situation and anticipate that the water level would go *below* that of the original beaker if the second beaker were *wider* instead of thinner.

Note that the operational knowing which predicts a certain physical situation ("the water level will go down") is *not* the same as the visual image one may be able to form of it. An image or a drawing, just like a gesture or a verbal sentence, is merely a symbolic expression through which a particular knowing becomes articulated or communicated. There is, however, no evidence to support the claim that a representational symbol must accompany every act of intelligent knowing such that a child's correct prediction of the water level is based on the child's visual imagination. On the contrary, we conclude that "understanding quantity" or "having the concept of quantity" is the same as having a particular operational structure (operation), whereas a verbal or an image expression is a secondary consequence. Once the operation is established in the development of a particular child, it is part of him and he functions according to it as naturally as he takes a step sideways to avoid an obstacle in front of him.

We have so far stressed the structure and the functioning of concepts as distinct from images or the usual verbal definitions. We have also briefly pointed out that concepts are not separately existing entities. I would like to say more on this point to correct our dictionary ways of thinking about concepts. The behavioral structures that make up the concepts are not single entities functioning separately side by side. Discursive language makes us analyze reality into separate parts and lay them out in a linear arrangement, one after the other. But we need not cramp our thinking about reality within the limitations imposed by the verbal medium. Even though we speak of concepts one by one, much as you will find them in a dictionary, we should realize that this separation is merely a manner of speaking.

The functioning of a behavioral scheme implies the functioning of the entire organism, the whole person. He alone exists and functions. When we focus on structures of knowing, we intentionally leave aside other aspects (e.g., motivational) which are always part of the total picture. But even when we limit our attention to the knowing aspect of behavior, we must realize that all knowing schemes are related to each other and none can function in splendid isolation. Depending on the generality of schemes, each scheme stands in a hierarchical, active relation to schemes above it and below it.

In fact, the distinguishing characteristic of strictly operational schemes is that they fit into total systems which are self-consistent and complete. Our minds can reflectively grasp the system and put it in logical form. This is the logician's job, but our concern is the child's spontaneously developing logic, rather than formal logic. Think of the child's two sentences: "Houses are in buildings"; "Houses are buildings." Here you have the verbalized concept of house in relation to building. The way the sentences are formed makes it impossible to fit the concepts of house and building into a coherent system. There is no reasonable way to get from one sentence to the other. The statements are not "reversible," in Piaget's terminology. Do you now understand why the characteristic of reversibility is a direct consequence of the functioning of a total logical system, and why Piaget stresses reversibility as the main criterion of operational thinking? Preoperational thinking lacks full reversibility, but this does not mean that preoperational concepts are not part of a structural totality; it merely means that preoperational structures do not form fully reversible systems.

In connection with the functional totality of a concept, it is worthwhile recalling that the development of schemes, from earlier to later levels of functioning, never means the disappearance of the old scheme and the simple substitution of a new scheme. Rather, organic development implies a progressive structuring so that later structures subsume earlier structures on a new level of functioning. For this reason we should not attach evaluative connotations to these levels. There is only one good way to sit down and that is by using sensorimotor schemes; no operational schemes by themselves would accomplish this task. Thus there are certain tasks that can be accomplished appropriately at different levels of functioning, depending on the nature of the task.

Finally, it would be a travesty if Piaget's theory, or my interpretation of it, were construed to suggest that *logical* objectivity is the only worthwile aspect of reality or is identical with reality. This is far from our intent, for logical intelligence is only *one* part of human functioning. It is an important part. It is the foundation on which logical objectivity rests. Quite literally, the human individual, on his way toward operational thinking, constructs objectivity; he does not simply register it from the start as a given fact. As important and valuable as logical thinking is, however, it is by no means the totality of life. In the previous letter, I referred purposely to musical constructions as differing from logical constructions. For there is intelligence in music, just as there is intelligence in art, in friendship, in love, and in social relations. Our minds cannot grasp the structures of these psychological realities in logical objectivity, but for all that, they exist for us and they exist objectively. I have attempted to present you with a perspective on thinking and human concepts that is much more inclusive than the familiar static notion of identifying concepts with verbal definititions. I think you would agree that a healthy view of logical thinking cannot but help restore a proper perspective on other aspects of human life. By limiting our immediate concern to the development of logical thinking, we are far from devaluating these other aspects.

However, this is enough food for your operational thinking. Best wishes until next time.

Sincerely yours,

operative versus figurative knowing

LETTER 5

Dear Teacher:

I am delighted with your response to the last letter. It seems you are getting the hang of Piaget's developmental theory. You talked over the behavioral samples with your colleagues and had quite a lively discussion. Your friend who teaches fourth grade did not believe that any of her children would give unreasonable responses to the question on houses and buildings. So she asked her class members individually and had the shock of her life. Only one girl out of nearly thirty children spontaneously gave an acceptable reply and reason. Moreover, fully one-third appeared quite impervious to corrections and never did realize the incongruency in their use of language.

You are right that we adults have little idea of the quality of thinking that goes on in the child. Children's activities are frequently hard to understand even in ordinary life. For practical purposes a mother and a father at home treat a young child appropriately enough. They are not really surprised when their eight-year-old boy runs out of the house, leaving all doors wide open, the television or the radio blaring away, even though he has been told any number of times to turn things off and close doors tightly. Nor when he puts a tray full of glasses in such a place that the next person who walks by must tip it over. Nor even when he plays with matches and

44

burns a hole in the tablecloth. We say that he did not think, that he was preoccupied with his immediate concerns, and that he did not foresee the consequences of his act. In other words, we admit that our frequent verbal admonitions were of no avail and hope that the practical experience of life will bring understanding where words have failed.

When teachers are faced with the inappropriate use of words, their immediate reaction is to remedy this situation by trying to teach the specific concept. If you have at all benefited from our discussion in the last letter, you can guess the underlying fallacy of "teaching a concept." It betrays a static view, as if a concept were an isolated bit of information which is memorized the way you recall a friend's birthday. However, the point at issue is not really bits of information. The children undoubtedly knew the usual meanings of the words "house" and "buildings." But they were not readily able to apply the appropriate meanings within a verbal context. There was a dearth not of words or information but of thinking. Having the children write sentences that use the word "house" in the two meanings of building and home would not change the thinking structure. If I understand you correctly, one of your colleagues suggested some such remedy. I was glad to hear that you considered it as probably useless. I would have gone further and said, "Definitely useless and probably harmful."

Apart from this, articulating new ideas in your own words by talking things over with others and constantly referring theoretical statements to actual examples are just about the two most necessary and effective means of making Piaget's or anyone else's ideas your own. Only then are you in a position to accept or reject them critically. Too many of us are satisfied with regurgitating general, unanalyzed statements. "Give me a concrete example" should be the first requirement of ourselves and of those who argue with us. And, by example, I mean relevant examples. For instance, it disturbs me that those who argue in favor of the important role of language in the development of thinking constantly come up with behavioral experiments of rote memory or perceptual discrimination, in which human thinking is at a minimum. To prove their point, they should provide examples where thinking is vigorously and obviously present. You also experienced something similar when your colleagues opposed you by providing concrete examples of thinking in school, for their examples were all taken from higher grade levels than the five-to-nine age group on which we are focusing our attention.

Do you know what happens when you or the children in your class are required to provide a concrete illustration or a rephrasing of some verbal statement expressing a new idea? By these activities one is forced to assimilate one's own particular illustration to the same structure to which one assimilated the new idea. To succeed in this task one must actively engage a structure of knowing—in short, one must think. The structure gives or, if you like, *is* the meaning of the total situation. If structure is absent, words become empty sequences of sound; one would be unable to produce illustrations or new articulations of something that has no meaning.

If a parrot, instead of saying his usual, "Good morning to you," should one day come out with "I am so glad you had a good night's rest," you would have good evidence that he had assimilated the original sound sequence to a particular structure of meaning—and, moreover, possessed linguistic competence. But since this only happens in fairy tales, we may rest assured that the parrot's structure underlying his speech is a sensorimotor scheme that is very accurate in accommodation but quite meager in assimilative power. It is only a perceptual assimilation that goes no further than the particular sound sequence and results in a more or less exact replica of the external intonation. On the other hand, a symbolic event is always assimilated to a structure that is related to a great variety of other structures and instances. Thus the ability to provide an illustration or a rephrasing demonstrates the degree to which one has assimilated the original verbal symbols in the first place.

Symbols, like adaptive actions, manifest structures of knowing. While symbols always refer to operational schemes, or at least to preoperational (i.e., operational in the wide sense) schemes, actions can be the product either of a sensori-motor or an operational scheme. To the parrot, the sound sequence has no symbolic character; it is what it perceptually is to the hearing organism and remains at that level. To a hearing organism who has some operational and also some linguistic competence, the perceived sound sequence is merely the material event which is assimilated to a structure of meaning. This structure enables the organism to comprehend and reproduce the symbol meaningfully or produce the meaning in other symbolic activities.

Let me follow my own advice and give an example of the difference in utilizing perceptual cues in sensorimotor and in operational behavior. An infant who knows his way around the home has assimilated local cues (primarily visual and tactual) and treats them for what they are: cues by which to move around. He is at the sensorimotor level. An eight-year-old child can assimilate the same cues to a more developed structure, the operational structure of coordinated space. He can therefore move around not only actually but symbolically. This may mean, in the particular instance, that he could form a visual image of his home, or that he could draw and recognize a diagram of the location, or, finally, that he could verbalize the position of certain spatial cues. In both cases the external reality provides the material content, and the assimilating structure of the organism gives it the appropriate meaning, such that the sensorimotor organism reacts adaptively to perceived cues whereas the operational child is capable of symbolizing the cues. Symbolization is thus a consequence of operational thinking.

It is important to keep in mind that operations and symbols are, at least theoretically, separate functions. This separation is differently described whether one focuses on the symbol or on the operation. Regarding the functioning of reversible operations, they are as such independent of symbols. I have no difficulty in postulating an operational situation where no symbolic activity is required. Recall here the examples given in Letter 3 concerning classifying a pile of blocks according to three dimensions of size, color, and shape. In Piaget's theory no symbol, verbal or imagined, need accompany the correct sorting into the appropriate spaces of the three overlapping hoops. This is not to say that symbolizing plays no role in operational thinking. It is merely to point to the possibility that they are separate functions and that operational thinking at times can take place without symbols (but then not without perception).

One can have, therefore, an operation without a symbol, but one cannot have a symbol without an operation. Regarding the functioning of symbols, the separation of symbol and operation can be conceptualized as a distinction between the material aspect and the meaning aspect of a symbol. The material aspect of a symbol more or less imitates some external reality, whereas the operational aspect gives symbolic meaning to the material content.

Now I must introduce two more terms which Piaget uses: figurative knowing and operative knowing. In common parlance, figurative is the opposite of literal and relates to the nonpresent, as in a figure of speech. Here, on the contrary, figurative refers to the present, static configuration of a thing. In the specialized sense in which we shall be using the term, *figurative knowing* is that aspect of knowing which focuses on the static configuration of given things as they appear to the senses. *Operative knowing,* on the other hand, "operates" on and transforms a given situation into a "form" (e.g., instance of a class, end-result of a construction, object to bypass) which is food for understanding and can be assimilated according to available schemes. Coming back to symbols, we can now see that the *material aspect* deals primarily with *figurative knowing* whereas the *meaning aspect* emphasizes *operative knowing.*

At the sensorimotor level all functioning is by definition toward perceptual events (sensory) and therefore figurative, but at the same time it is entirely action-oriented (motor) and therefore operative. For the sensorimotor organism, to perceive something is to behave motorically in respect to it. Thus figurative and operative aspects are organically united. The conceptual separation of figurative and operative knowing becomes meaningful only with the achievement of operational structures that enable a person to know without externally acting. This possibility is particularly evident in symbol formation, for in symbol formation we are dealing with behavior that *uses some figurative (material) knowing in the service of operative (meaning) knowing.*

Apart from the symbolic competence, the operational capacity endows us with the possibility of knowing things from various perspectives. Take this ubiquitous English verb "to know" and consider what "to know Piaget" can mean. This knowledge can range from the knowing of a four-year-old child who has been questioned by Monsieur Piaget on some preoperational problem all the way to the knowledge of the scholar who has systematically assimilated Piaget's theory. Having once dissociated the internal scheme from the appropriate external act, the person with an operational scheme becomes free to employ it in a given event to varying degrees.

At the operational level the distinction between figurative and operative becomes important because the respective contributions of the figurative and the operative aspects are no longer organically determined. *One can know something with "more" or "less" understanding.* An operational knowing at the level of "I know what a TV is" may simply reflect on the sensorimotor knowledge of a television set. That is, a person making this statement knows some perceptual characteristics and some appropriate motor reactions regarding the television; he may know that it is something to turn on or off, to sit in front of and watch. This meager operational knowing focuses primarily on perceptual, figurative aspects (e.g., shape and size of the television, location of controls). While some *low-level operative* functioning underlies this largely figurative knowing, we should differentiate it from a *high-level operative* knowing about a television set. Here we refer to the individual who comprehends the functioning of a set, who knows how it is constructed and how it works.

You recall what was said at the beginning of our correspondence about knowing. I suggested as a general starting point in our investigation that we consider knowing as related to the construction and functioning of the known thing. Knowing, true to its character, is not a passive contemplation of a static thing out there. It is a dialectic process by which environmental data are transformed and assimilated according to the knower's subjective structures. In turn, through the knowing organism the objective environment is constituted as something toward which the organism can function in an adaptive, meaningful manner. In this interplay of organism and environment, knowing is not a factor added to preconstituted elements and somehow connecting one with the other. Rather, it is the structuring, organizing aspect of all organic functioning.

Sensorimotor functioning has been described as an increasingly more adaptive capacity for action toward the environment. It manifests what Piaget calls a logic of action and for the same reason is referred to as practical intelligence. At this level there exists no ground for separating action from perception because knowing the configuration of a thing is equivalent to reacting motorically toward it. With the transition to the operational capacity this natural equilibration between acting and knowing is beginning to be broken.

The child begins to manifest his knowing of a thing even without direct action on the thing. Instead of assimilating a situation to a practical action scheme, the child older than two is capable of assimilation to a preoperational scheme, notably the object scheme. In this manner a child manifests his first "nonpractical" knowing. His assimilation of things in the environment to the object scheme means that he knows that there is a chair, a table, food, mother, daddy, a hand, a foot, shoes, socks, and so on.

Note the character of this budding knowledge. It is operational insofar as it is the knowing of an object, but otherwise it is at first indistinguishable from sensorimotor knowing. Operationally, it is a knowing that simply registers a particular thing out there. The two-year-old child does not understand operationally anything else about the thing; he does not know it as an instance of a class, in relation to other things, how it is made, or what its function is. On all these counts the knowing is still only a practical know-how, and as such it is tied to specific personal actions; it is "egocentric" to an extreme degree. From an operational perspective, therefore, preoperational knowing begins with a heavy focus on the personally experienced configuration of things. It requires a development of many years before the child's operational knowing becomes sufficiently operative (transforming) to transcend the figurative aspect which derives from personal experience.

Progress during the preoperational period is therefore primarily an increase in operativity. From a figurative aspect the small child's knowing of his plate is about as good as it may ever be, but his operative knowing concerning a plate, its use and construction, is steadily increasing. By the time or shortly after the child goes to kindergarten, his operative knowing takes on for the first time a stable character in the strict operations of the concrete-operational period. During the next few years occurs the last period of intellectual development, which is nothing more than a continuous increase in operative thinking toward the formal operational stage. An education that desires to foster and nourish the growth of intelligence will pay particular attention to those activities that challenge operative thinking. In order to accomplish this, you as a teacher must first appreciate the difference between figurative and operative aspects of knowing. You must understand that intelligence does not develop from the figurative aspect of knowing but from the operative activity by way of what we have called formal abstraction.

Let me recapitulate and clarify the terminology, which is a little confusing. On the one hand, Piaget refers to three broad stages of the developing intelligence: (1) sensorimotor; (2a) preoperational and (2b) concrete operational; and (3) formal operational. The distinction between operative and figurative is on a different plane and refers to aspects of the known object. Operative knowing emphasizes the action aspect that transforms given data in order to assimilate them to available general structures. Figurative knowing emphasizes the aspect which focuses on the particular configuration of given data. The distinction is unimportant at the sensorimotor stage, when these two aspects are organically united. However, during and after the preoperational substage, intellectual development means primarily a gradual increase in operative knowing with respect to figurative knowing. Therefore, the distinction between figurative and operative knowing helps us particularly in two situations: first, in the case of symbolic behavior, which always has a *material* (figurative) aspect and a *meaning* (operative) aspect; and second, in the case of operative knowing, which can take place at a *low level* (primarily figurative) or at a *high level.* Not just any symbol use, nor just any knowing, provides the occasion for intellectual growth. Only high-level operative knowing or high-level operative symbol use is challenging as food for intellectual expansion.

I mentioned at the beginning of this letter that symbols always have a figurative and an operative aspect. The operative aspect gives meaning to symbols, whether we consider the recognition or the production of symbols. A symbol—for example, a word or a drawing—can be recognized as meaningful only if the individual has an operative scheme to which the symbol is assimilated. In a similar manner, the symbol can be produced or reproduced only by an individual with an underlying operative scheme. The operative scheme is the referent, the direct meaning of the symbol.

The figurative or material aspect of the symbol is that by which a symbol is a thing, a particular movement, a particular sound sequence, a particular visual configuration. Here are some examples: "come" symbolized in a gesture of pointing in the direction of one's body; "hurry" symbolized as an articulated (verbal) sound; "go in a certain direction" symbolized in a gesture that outlines the particular direction to be taken, for example, first a little to the left side, then a sharp turn right, and finally straight toward the goal. If we leave discussion of verbal language for another time and ask where these movements come from, the answer, according to Piaget's observations, is that they derive from real actions. They imitate schematically sensorimotor actions.

Imitation is built into sensorimotor actions. The scheme of grasping, as it accommodates to each differently shaped thing, imitates the particular outline of the grasped thing. This imitation is an integral part of the sensorimotor act. At the operational stage, however, this imitative and accommodative movement can get detached from the act so as to become the figurative material for a symbolic act. Thus a physical movement, which served an actual physical purpose at the sensorimotor level (e.g., to pull something to oneself), now serves as the symbolic material to be used in an operational scheme.

Consider this example: Some part of the external movement of throwing a ball (a sensorimotor act) is used by the knowing child (knowing is an operational act) to symbolize that knowing. In other words, a three-year-old child who thinks of the ball and needs to communicate to others something about the ball may use the external gesture to represent the internal operational scheme. In this case the external gesture is the figurative aspect, whereas the internal scheme is the operative aspect of the symbolic act. In Piaget's terms, the external movement of throwing is assimilated to the operational scheme of throwing. The scheme gives meaning to the external movement.

If you have followed me so far, we can go one step further. The examples up to now have been of symbols that are externally observable. What about symbols that are within one's own skin, such as internally felt movements? What about internal images—visual, auditory, or of some other sense modality? What about a picture or a drawing which represents externally some image within the person? On this point Piaget suggests the following rather straightforward solution. An external gesture differs from an external sensorimotor act in terms of quantity; that is, the gesture is a partial act. And an internal image differs from an external gesture in terms of quantity; that is, the image is a diminutive gesture. The external gesture of throwing a ball becomes a covert muscle movement which the thinking individual may himself experience as a slight tension in his muscles or as an internal visual image of a thrown ball. The *covert* kinesthetic (motor) or visual *image* is essentially the same as the *overt gesture*. In other words, it is also a symbol. As a symbol it implies an operational scheme of knowing that gives it meaning (that is its operative aspect), and it includes an actual, even though not externally observable, movement (that is its figurative aspect). The figurative aspect of a symbol has, therefore, a physical status of existence (an actual motoric act, whether external or internal) while the operative aspect is simply the knowing scheme, which has no reality status apart from the functioning organism.

This may all sound very abstract to you, and you may wonder why I keep stressing the distinction between figurative and operative and why I derive figurative from an external, physical act and operative from an internal structure. My answer to this follows: Our traditional notions about thinking and symbols have been thoroughly warped by centuries of pseudo-scientific positivism (only things that can be quantified exist) and mechanistic causality (all science must ulti- mately be reducible to mechanical laws of physics). If traditional theories of intelligence and learning were adequate and their educational applications were successful in practice, we would not be forced to question these theories. Make no mistake about the influence of theoretical ideas. The simplest explanations of gravity, which today any nine-year-old child can sufficiently grasp, seemed obscure abstractions and farfetched hypotheses to scholars who were contemporaries of Galileo or Newton. Once we have a new perspective, everything falls easily into place. What I propose to you here is nothing short of a Copernican revolution regarding intelligence, learning, and symbols. It should turn our theories, and consequently our practice, upside down.

According to the old tradition, symbols were the carriers of meaning. The internal image of throwing a ball was adduced as an explanation for the phenomenon of internally knowing a ball. Now Piaget suggests that the relation be completely reversed, that the image as a symbol requires an explanation and that the knowing alone can explain the symbolic character. Far from the symbols by themselves explaining the knowing, it is the knowing that is required to explain the symbol. Although this sounds simple enough, you cannot expect that a short sentence like the preceding one is all that is needed to turn our tradition around.

When you apply the new perspective to educational purposes, you can appreciate how "abstract" theories can have very practical results. If symbols are considered to be the principal carriers of meaning, the excessive emphasis on language and reading becomes understandable. What better way to strengthen "meaning" than to focus on its principal determiner? What are we saying? Does it make sense to talk of "strengthening meaning"? Of course it does not. This is precisely the point. Educators hope that somehow, by focusing on symbols and on their meanings, they automatically focus on thinking. But this is not the case. Teachers themselves realize that there is no built-in transfer from symbolic meaning to thinking. When we stress symbolic or verbal configurations, particularly during the ages of early elementary school, we engage the child in what we called low-level operative functioning. It was for this reason that elementary teachers did not know how to answer my innocent questioning about occasions in school that challenge thinking.

As your teacher friend reported, having nine-year-old children focus on the *meaning* of houses and buildings will not readily make them see that "all houses are buildings" but only "some buildings are houses." These *thinking* relationships are not part of symbolic meanings, but these relations of thinking determine the reasonable use of language.

Philosophers also far prefer to busy themselves with meanings than with thinking. Many make the claim that thinking is nothing but a manipulation of meanings expressed in symbols. To all these people we must point out that they fail to analyze adequately the concept of symbol. They subtly shift from the figurative aspect of a symbol to the operative aspect without realizing it. My whole contention is that theories of thinking must get away from preoccupation with the figurative aspect of knowing and focus on the operative aspect of knowing, which is thinking.

Now, what has all this to do with educators? It forces a fundamental question which it is impossible even to pose within the framework of traditional theories. Since symbols combine both figurative and operative aspects, we educators must have a clear idea whether a specific symbolic activity strengthens one or the other aspect. We can not even ask this question until we realize that these two aspects exist. To realize the operative aspect as distinct from the figurative needs a constant effort on our part, for the simple reason that a static thing is easier to describe and to become aware of than a constructive activity.

The slow and laborious development of the child, which consists essentially in an increasingly greater degree of operative functioning, should have made the distinction between figurative and operative rather obvious to a systematic observer of knowing. However, apart from Piaget, theorists of thinking have not bothered to look to the child and to the biological beginning, but instead have started their theorizing at the end. Seeing that in mature life one engages in challenging thinking most typically through the use of verbal symbols, they identified thinking and language in practice and thus failed to see the important difference between the figurative or low-level operative knowing of a symbol and the high-level, operative use of it.

Let me try to summarize this difficult letter to help you grasp the more important points. When knowing becomes dissociated from an accommodation to a full external action, it is beginning to become operational (in the wide sense). Preoperational thinking reflects on, or abstracts from, sensorimotor knowing, starting with the personally experienced action aspects and gradually transcending these by the development of fully reversible operations. These operations are the framework within which stable, objective concepts and logical reasoning are established. The figurative aspect of knowing relates to specific configurations of external acts or things; the operative aspect relates to the operations that transform and assimilate given data according to the operations' own logical structure. Symbols have a figurative aspect, which derives from personal, external actions, and an operative aspect, which gives symbolic meaning to the actions. Intellectual growth is most conspicuously observed in a gradual overcoming of egocentric, figurative perspectives (whether in symbolic or nonsymbolic behavior) by means of operative structures. Symbols are used according to the level of available operative structures—frequently below the level but never above it. In early childhood, symbolic use does not by itself challenge operative structures; it is frequently a low-level operative activity and is therefore not usually an occasion for intellectual growth. It may even reinforce the egocentric figurative perspective that exists in the child's thinking, if the operative aspect of the overall situation is of no interest to the child.

I am afraid I have summarized more than was actually discussed in this letter. At least I know that I can safely start the next letter with a fuller explanation of the last two sentences. They were written with particular reference to the "formal" as distinct from the spontaneous use of language and can, therefore, aptly introduce the topic of language and thinking. I will try to answer your immediate questions as best I can. Perhaps you can defer some until the next letter, in which I will focus on the most explicit symbol system—verbal language. Many issues that could be raised at this point will come up again and be discussed in connection with language.

Best wishes, and please continue your discussion with your colleagues.

Cordially yours,

the role of language in thinking

Dear Teacher:

I will respond to your three questions one at a time.

1. If internal symbols derive from external movements, what are the external movements that lead to an internal visual image? In answering this question you should be familiar with Piaget's work on perception. Briefly, he considers perception to be not a static copy on the part of the sense modality but an active functioning of the total organism. It is an organized encounter with a situation present to the sensing organism. Underlying the organizing activity are schemes of knowing, perceptual schemes, which the organism accommodates to the given data and to which these data are assimilated. For instance, the visual gaze vis-à-vis a given object— say, a car—is not the same in a one-year-old, a three-year-old, and a five-year-old child. Literally, children at different ages "perceive" the car differently, as can be observed in the way they coordinate eye movements in a rapid succession of "centrations" and "decentrations." Although we do not commonly call them "movements," these coordinating shifts of sensory focusing are truly a motoric functioning. Piaget holds that they form the material on which internal images rest, whereas the meaning of images is based on an operational knowing (say, of a car) that is no longer tied to an external act.

56

2. What exactly is the difference between operative and operational? Operative is the wider concept. It expresses the action aspect of knowing, including both operational and sensorimotor at all stages, insofar as knowing acts on things and transforms them into things of action or objects of understanding. Operational, on the other hand, is a stage-specific characteristic of intelligent knowing and excludes sonsorimotor activities. Operative knowing, as distinct from figurative knowing, emphasizes the action aspect of all knowing. Operational intelligence makes it possible for the individual to direct his attention to the static aspects of a thing with only a minimum of active understanding. Such a knowing is here called figurative (or low-level operative) in the sense that knowing focuses on, or stops short at, the static content (configuration) of the known event. Figurative knowing never occurs in isolation because some operative aspects must be present in all knowing, as I pointed out above in connection with perceptual schemes. Moreover, you should not think of figurative knowing as an aspect that is intrinsically inferior to operative knowing. At times figurative knowing is very appropriate. Nor is it desirable that children or adults constantly function at a high operative level. Our concern here is merely to remind ourselves that some school tasks, such as learning to read, are primarily figurative and low-level operative; that is, they rarely use available operative structures to full capacity.

3. Do symbols alone have meanings? Don't signals and even external acts have meaning? Why restrict meaning to operational symbols? Yours is partly a semantic question; that is, what "meaning" do you wish to give to the word "meaning?" Signals have meanings since they are cues for action, but they are tied to action. They have no meaning apart from the action; they have, as Piaget says, an "undifferentiated" meaning. A symbol, however, is a "differentiated" sign. The meaning of the symbol is not tied to specific external actions, but refers directly to a knowing. To summarize the distinction, signal behavior is a sensorimotor reaction to a sign, whereas symbol behavior is an operational response (knowing) to a sign. Finally, when you hear expressions like "An act like breathing has meaning," you should realize that the word in this context differs from the meaning of a sign. "Meaningful" here means functional, adaptive, comprehensible in itself, quite the opposite from the meaning of a symbol, which represents and points toward something else.

The last point is an apt illustration of the intricacies into which verbal language forces us. If we educated adults have trouble analyzing the different meanings behind linguistically identical expressions ("Breathing has meaning"; "The green traffic light has meaning"), how can anyone seriously suggest that language is the appropriate, if not indispensable, tool for the development of thinking? Indeed, this is a good illustration of my contention that *thinking* is the indispensable tool for using language appropriately.

When we began our search for a suitable method to investigate thinking, a biological, developmental approach seemed adequate and provided a fruitful perspective. We will now proceed similarly with regard to the language of society.

From the viewpoint of adult intelligence, Piaget observed that operational thinking, once it is developed and approaches a mature stage, takes on increasingly the form of propositions. The reality to which mature thinking structures correspond is no longer found in the realm of concrete encounters with the physical world but in a realm that becomes, when symbolized, the formal language of reason and science. With reference to this formalized logic, as distinct from spontaneous logic, Piaget characterizes the final stage of intellectual development as *formal operational* whereas the previous stage is termed *concrete operational.* We can, therefore, come to the following important conclusion. *Verbal statements and propositions come into their own as primary nourishment of the child's intelligence as he is getting close to formal operational functioning.* This means that once the intelligence has, as it were, grown up—and not earlier—it then becomes ready to feed and expand on verbal material.

However, when we take the child's viewpoint, we observe that language is as much a part of the physical environment as streets with their traffic, as the changes of day and night. It is, of course, closely linked to the presence of other people and in this sense can be called part of the social environment. During the sensorimotor period the infant does not appear to pay special attention to linguistic sounds. A child born deaf to all sound does not at first act differently from a hearing child. For this reason deafness is not readily discovered before the age when language should emerge.

When the child begins to enter the preoperational stage, there appear simultaneously the first manifestations of operational knowledge, of symbolic behavior in the form of gestures and play, and of linguistic comprehension. It was one of Piaget's most ingenious insights to point to the similarity between linguistic and other symbolic activities. In fact, for the child language is just one of the different forms in which his symbolic ability becomes manifest. To realize the similarity between language and other symbols, recall how symbols come about.

Let us say that a two-year-old child watches the unloading of some big, heavy steel bars that are carried from a truck to near a building site. If we observe the child closely as he watches the men unloading, we will notice the child's gestures which accompany his watching of the workmen. With fingers spread wide open as if to hold a large thing, the child moves his arms along in imitation of the observed carrying. These outward imitative movements form part of the ac-commodation aspect of the total perceptual situation. The assimila-tion aspect consists in the child's capacity to structure the event, that is, to know something about what is going on. This knowing may be nothing more than "men carrying something big and heavy." Some hours later at home the child may be seen using similar gestures in the absence of the model. This is the child's way of expressing to himself or to others his knowing about something interesting that happened to him. We describe this behavior as symbolic imitation. All symbolic behavior includes some imitation of real events. In the previous letter the imitative aspect of a symbol was called the figura-tive, material aspect of a symbol. The operative aspect of the sym-bolic imitation, however, is the same operative scheme by which the child assimilated the original perceptual situation.

Can I restate the same situation once more? The child watches an interesting sight. In Piaget's language, he assimilates an event to his sensorimotor and preoperational schemes and accommodates the schemes to the event. This accommodation becomes in part visible by overt imitation of real configurations. Later, in the absence of the event, the child makes the event present (represents it) by means of the figurative gestures which accompanied his watching. These ges-tures are symbolic to the child. Underlying the gestures and giving meaning to them are the same operational schemes by which the child structured the original event.

Now let us suppose that during the child's intent observation of the men, an adult was present and verbalized the interest of the child in some way: "Yes, the bars are big and heavy, aren't they? Big, big and heavy." These verbal sounds are already familiar to the child. They form part of the environment, as do the men, steel bars, and so on. Perhaps the child can be heard imitating the sounds of the speaker. In any case, if some time later he recalls this event by repeating something like "big . . . 'evy," we can say the same thing about the words we said about the gestures. The child imitates some figurative part of the interesting situation as a symbol by which to manifest his original knowing.

Does the child's knowing increase on account of symbol representation? Not really. On what basis would symbolic repetition of a situation improve knowing of the situation? A child who plays policeman manifests his knowing of policemen by symbolic gestures. He obviously enjoys acting out this knowing but it is not at all clear that playing policeman helps him grow in knowledge of a policeman's function. Growth of knowing at this young age level requires *actual contact.* Symbolic contact merely replays existing knowing according to the child's level of development.

All this is equally true for the linguistic symbol. The child's operative knowing is not challenged simply on account of using verbal symbols. Although a three-year-old child may say a hundred times, "Daddy going to work at university," the child's knowing of the nature of work or of a university is really quite unaffected by these verbal statements. For the child language is not some abstract proposition which challenges the intelligence—as it can in the formal operational stage—but is of the same stuff as his play, his gestures, and his images.

We discussed in the previous letter and in the first question of this letter that an image, according to Piaget, is the internalized motor functioning of imitative movement. It may be experienced as kinesthetic, as auditory, or frequently as visual image. As the child develops, his overt gestures accompanying his knowing behavior become less obvious. Just as every human child plays in *overt* symbolic activity manifesting his knowing, so does he increasingly enjoy an active life of fantasy and images in *covert* symbolic activity.

In the preoperational period, a child's knowing is only partially freed from personal overt experience. The dependence of his knowing on this experience is primarily observed in the child's too great reliance on his own symbols. During the period the child thinks "in images." In this connection I recall the four-year-old youngster with whom my colleague played baseball. The child missed the ball thrown to him by his father and it ended up behind the rosebushes. The boy ran after it, stopped short of the rosebush, knelt down, and stretched out his right hand as if grasping an imaginary ball and pulling it to himself by a series of careful movements. Having done this, he proceeded to the "real" rosebush and carefully got the ball. I watched this performance one Sunday afternoon five or six times. Each time, as the child approached the rosebush, he reminded himself to be careful by the symbolic gestures just described. You can be sure that this child's thinking about getting a ball from behind the rose bushes was strongly dependent on his own experience.

Perhaps the child experienced an internal image of the bush while he acted; perhaps he did not. Nobody really knows; hence the experience of images is not easily defined. What is obvious is that the child at the preoperational level thinks consistently *in terms of his own experience*. This has two results. First, the personal experience is frequently acted out by gestures or incipient movements. The "acting out" of knowledge is observed in symbolic behavior, play, language, images, dreams. Second, the child's own experience typically colors his thinking and makes it appear immature from the viewpoint of adult reason.

The different kinds of symbolic behavior have one thing in common: the knowing child makes use of external activity in the service of symbolic representation. I apologize for using this rather awkward phrasing. But note what happens if I simply said the child uses the symbols to represent his knowing. This could imply that his knowledge resides in the symbolic representation. This may again seem a rather picayune difference. But wait a minute.

Does it not seem quite natural to you to call knowing an internal representation? Would you not feel quite comfortable if I spoke of representational knowing every time I mentioned operational knowing? And if I asked you, what do you mean by representational knowing, you would reply, a kind of internal knowing of external things by means of an internal representation of these things. In other words, you would have no objection to the statement that knowing is a representative copy of things outside; that the human child, as he grows older, becomes capable of internalizing this copy so that eventually he is capable of internal, representational knowing.

Unfortunately, our verbal language permits us to say all these things in well-formed, familiar-sounding sentences. It therefore requires an almost heroic effort of thinking on our part to realize the basic fallacy in this way of talking. Piaget's revolution is directed precisely against these habits of language without thinking. It is much easier to change an opponent's viewpoint when his argument is well articulated than when we battle against unanalyzed assumptions that are vaguely expressed. Concerning the points raised in the paragraph above, you would stop and ask for clarifications. If representational knowing resides in symbolic representation, what exactly does representation mean? Does it refer to an internal image or some internal brain process? And is this internal something really knowing? If this were the case we would be able to get hold of knowing as a nice neat thing, right there in the internal process which copies reality; these internal codes or representations would be the carriers of knowing and meaning.

Piaget, however, points out that knowing is never a figurative, static thing or pattern, inside or outside the human skin, and that figurative imitations of external things, outside or inside the human skin, are at best symbols that get their meaning from knowing. If representational knowing implies a knowing that resides in a figurative pattern, this implication would be sheer nonsense for Piaget's theory of operative knowing. But he can speak of representational knowing in the sense that a person beyond the sensorimotor stage is capable of representation, that is, of producing and comprehending a figurative pattern as an operative symbol.

If you can accept the fact that symbols, overt or internal, carry meaning not in themselves but only insofar as they depend on the knowing scheme of the individual who uses them, it becomes quite unreasonable to expect that through symbols, of themselves, knowing will be strengthened. Observe young children at play. Watch how they symbolize planes and cars, buildings and roads. I am not saying that this is a useless activity, far from it. I am merely asserting that the child's knowing of planes, cars, buildings, and roads is not automatically furthered by this play. Piaget suggests that in early play assimilation prevails over accommodation; that is, the child employs the materials not for what they are in themselves, but insofar as they as symbols can be incorporated into the child's available knowing schemes. Here is a clear example of a differentiated sign; the child obviously knows that a box is not a building, but he can readily use a box as a symbolic representation of a building. By playing building he exercises his symbolic capacity. He may derive from it all kinds of functional and emotional satisfaction, but he does not improve his knowing vis-à-vis the box, for he is purposely not interested in the box as a box but only insofar as it provides the material for representing a building. Nor does symbolic play give him the opportunity to improve his knowing of a building. For this he would need contact with a real building. You can even see that the preoccupation with his personal representation of a building could hinder progress in his understanding of the real building if for some reason he remains attached to the figurative symbol rather than the operative reality.

May I recapitulate the developmental perspective on symbolic representation? We have observed a preoperational knowing that at the start is predominantly descriptive and functions in terms of images but gradually becomes more and more operative and to this extent transcends the symbolic images. As I said before, the chief difference between your knowing of a building and a four-year-old child's knowing is not the presence or absence of a particular image. Both of you may make use of the same figurative pattern. The difference lies in the way the image contributes to the knowing. In the three-year-old it dominates knowing and makes it immature and egocentric. In the adult, however, the knowing dominates the image and uses it for purposes of attention or as a pictorial sample.

We seem to have wandered off from our main topic, language. But this is not really the case, if you realize that everything that has been said regarding symbol, image, and representation is fully applicable to language. Language is acquired by the child through meaningful imitation, just as are motoric gestures. I say "meaningful" to stress again the fact that imitation, though it may at times appear to be a copy of an external model, is never merely a passive copy; for imitation is always linked to an active scheme of knowing even though the knowing may not be very profound.

Exactly like a gesture, language too can become internalized—that is, fragmentary and spoken subvocally. Whereas for gestures and movements that are internalized we use the generic term "image," internalized language is often called "inner language." That seems to set language apart from other symbols, but is that a justifiable conclusion? The linguistic symbol does not occupy a privileged position in the child's symbolic repertory; it is treated as egocentrically as any visual or kinesthetic symbol. Anybody who systematically observes the way children use language can attest to the accuracy of this statement. It is hardly necessary to illustrate here that in the young child language falls squarely into the category of mental image and has all the characteristics of this category: it is personal, it is particular, it is figurative, it tends to dominate operative thinking.

The earliest use of language, just like the early use of gestures, is, appropriately enough, limited to a kind of social communication that is hardly above the level of which some higher animals are capable. It is only natural that the transition from the signal behavior of the sensorimotor period to the symbol behavior of the operational period should be quite gradual and imperceptible. The first words are usually uttered in closest proximity to the situation to which the child's knowing is directed. It takes a long time before the child can detach words from the appropriate external action. Ask a two- to three-year-old child to repeat after you, "I jump," and you will notice that in repeating the words the child jumps. Ask the child to repeat, "Sit down," he will immediately move toward sitting and, if a chair is available, he will actually sit down. Similar observations can be made with regard to the child's tendency to accompany his actions with a descriptive verbal commentary ("I run," "I knock," etc.).

Consider our earlier example of the boy pulling the ball out of the bushes. From the viewpoint of knowing, there is no difference between the child's making the motoric gesture or speaking some audible words about being very careful. Both the words and the gestures are imitations of external figurative patterns and both are assimilated to the child's knowing schemes of "being careful." The examples just given demonstrate clearly that for the child the verbal sound sequence "Sit down" is as much a figurative part of the sit-down event as the actual movements of sitting down. Only as the child's operative knowing increases and he understands that the *object* of sitting down is independent from the particular *action* of sitting down, will he be capable of using a symbol (visual, kinesthetic, or verbal) more freely and objectively.

We adults are frequently misled by the verbal skill of children and attribute to them a knowing of which the children are quite incapable. The little three-year-old girl may be quite capable of comprehending or expressing the verbal sentence, "Water is boiling on the stove," but let us not impute to her any operative knowing about the physical process of boiling. The child's verbal expression as a symbol is assimilated to her knowing of the water-boiling event. Her knowing is on a very low operative level, only barely above the knowing of a dog who keeps away from something hot. Yet it is above sensorimotor knowing for the very reason that the child can reflect on the situation as a known object (object formation) and can represent it by means of a figurative pattern (symbol formation).

Even at an age when a child has been in school for some years the operative comprehension of language is well below what we would superficially impute to him. For example, recall the nine-year-old child's inability to deal with such a simple problem as clarifying in his own mind the different senses of "house" and "building." This child could manage, piece by piece, different shades of meanings ("Houses are homes," "Houses are buildings"), but when confronted with conflicting verbal expressions, he could not spontaneously sift out the appropriate meanings.

We are also easily impressed by the child's mastery of the grammatical aspect of language; we think that he "knows" the linguistic rules from the fact that he "even speaks according to them." But is implicit knowing of rules, manifest in linguistic skills, really such an intellectual accomplishment? Is it so different from the "perceptual" rules of judging distances or the "social" rules of conduct? To acquire *implicit* rules for manipulating perceptual elements, for ordering and combining them, is a low-level operative skill compared to the high-level *explicit* operative skill of comprehending order or of combinatorial thinking. A young child's knowing of grammatical rules is comparable to an implicit knowing and is not the formal knowing of a person who studies grammar.

The general conclusion which I press on you is not to exaggerate the role of language in the development of thinking. I know that purely theoretical arguments will never convince a person who is committed to an opposing position. I know that the proposition about the dispensable role of language goes contrary to just about everything that experts in psychology and education hold and preach. To them I say: You have had your chance. You have sold the public a bill of fare that is indigestible to the common child.

You ask me how I can be so sure that verbal language does not make a vital contribution to the development of intelligence. Have I ever seen a child whose intellect developed normally without the help of language? This is, of course, an unfair question. You might just as well say that the heart or the air are vital determiners of intellectual growth since without them there would be no organism to develop. But I accept your challenge. Yes, I have seen and carefully observed not just one, but many hundreds of children who grow up without the opportunity to acquire linguistic skill in the ordinary way. I refer to children who are born with a profound hearing loss.

Here you have children who cannot participate in the linguistic environment but are otherwise unimpeded. The result? They find it exceedingly hard to learn to know the language of society. (I mean here knowing the language, not just speaking and lipreading. The last skill in particular is an exceptional ability. Even among deaf people who know the English language as well as you and I, it is as rare as the mastery associated with concert pianists.) Many deaf children attend special schools from the time they are three or four years old. By the time they are eight years old, most of them are able to read a few words and a few simple sentences. However, the difference in linguistic knowledge between any hearing youngster of similar age and the typical deaf youngster is like night and day. There is no need for any statistical tools. The hearing child knows language; that is, he masters the intricate set of linguistic rules together with a vocabulary of many thousand words and spontaneously applies this mastery in an infinite variety of situations. Over against this wealth of knowing, one cannot seriously entertain the notion that the laboriously acquired skill of a few words could produce in deaf children what the hearing child's language is proposed to accomplish. If verbal language is of vital importance for the development of the intelligence in an eight-year-old hearing child, the relative absence of verbal language in an eight-year-old deaf child should vitally impair the child's intellectual development. But this is not the case, as our research has clearly demonstrated.

There are still some deaf children who are kept away from school and are discovered only when they are well past early childhood. I worked with such a child a few months ago, a 13-year-old boy who had never been in a school before. He literally did not know a word of any social language. Yet I had no difficulty introducing him in a few hours to the logical symbols I will describe to you in another letter. Whatever other deficiencies in him or other deaf youngsters, only a person determined not to face facts can continue to hold that the language of society is of indispensable importance in the development of thinking.

What, then, is the role of language? Surely I do not consider language an unnecessary luxury. I wish I could say in a few words something that could do justice to so vast a topic. However, every scientist must limit the field under study. His statements should not be projected outside the carefully delimited field of investigation. Piaget studied one limited area of life, the spontaneous growth of the capacity for scientific thinking which turns out to be the logical aspect of human intelligence. On this topic he came to the conclusion that verbal language is not the stuff of which logical thinking is made, is not the food on which early logical thinking grows.

Piaget suggests two further points that have already been mentioned. First, he asserts that the structures of formal operations are suitable for making critical use of the linguistic symbol system. Although earlier structures of the growing intelligence are not capable of fully dominating linguistic habits,verbal language becomes the proper medium to stimulate and express thinking *after* the establishment of thinking structures close to the formal operational stage. The second point refers to the role of language at earlier levels of intellectual development. Here language shares a common role with other symbolic instruments. It remains, therefore, to provide an overview of the role of symbols. This gives me an additional opportunity to clarify misunderstandings that invariably arise when something contrary to common but largely unanalyzed assumptions is proposed.

Some people listen to the proposition that there can be thinking without language and then conclude that I thereby advocate the possibility that thinking can develop without symbols at all. Other people as you pointed out to me, interpret the proposal to mean that I believe language has no function at all, at least at early age levels. Of course I do not hold either of these opinions. It is evident to anyone seriously following Piaget's theory that symbolic behavior is an indispensable concomitant of preoperational thinking. One could actually characterize preoperational thinking as thinking in terms of symbols. But note that such a statement does not mean that the symbols *are* the thinking, or that the symbols in themselves carry the meaning of the thinking process. Preoperational thinking in terms of symbols means that symbols are present and needed and that their supporting presence limits the functioning of operative thinking.

The child gets his symbols from the external aspects of the environment. He imitates specific movements, specific external patterns or functions, and when he internalizes these imitations they become internal images. These form his internal world of symbols. All behavior that goes under the term "symbolic" draws its sustenance from there. Symbolic behavior includes the vast spectrum of human activities that do not have as their immediate object either a practical goal or theoretical knowing. Here we have play, dreams, social customs, art, music, religion, language, and so on.

The verbal language of the society forms, of course, an important part of the environment, a part that is specifically geared to become a symbolic instrument and a particularly apt instrument of social communication and socialization. On these three counts language plays a unique role and functions from the earliest age level to shape the personality of the growing infant. It plays a role in the infant's social and symbolic life insofar as it transmits to the child social and symbolic values, attitudes, commitments. It is part of the process by which the child assimilates society's style of life and conduct, moral and political values. It is the indispensable vehicle through which he learns the folklore and stories surrounding the history and culture of his society. And last but not least, it is the ready instrument through which the child communicates with his parents, his peers, and his elders.

Is this not enough? If I limit the role of language with regard to the development of thinking, am I implying it has no other role? I, for my part, do not hold that the fullness of human life is exhausted by logical thinking. Moreover, I stress that the environment (and language is part of the environment) has, of course, an effect on intellectual growth. The physical and social environments are necessary and can support or depress thinking, even though the stuff of operational thinking does not derive from the environment. And I conclude by suggesting that language does become the appropriate means in which logical thinking in its most mature form is expressed.

Where Piaget falls afoul of the strictures of so many of his contemporaries is in his firm conviction that symbols, including verbal language, by their own activities do not go beyond the level of the functioning of which they are a part. If we want to "go beyond," we must remember that in intellectual development "going beyond" is "formal abstraction." This abstraction, as I have already mentioned, belongs to the operative aspect of functioning. It requires the active assimilation and accommodation of those knowing schemes that challenge the *full* capacity of the particular thinking organism.

It is, of course, possible to have a functioning of schemes that activates *less* than the full capacity of the available operative structures. When this happens, we have low-level operative functioning, and there is no "going beyond." This is the case in many—indeed, in most—of our daily activities, which proceed according to habitual behavior patterns, and in many behaviors that focus on other than the logical aspects of a situation. It is also the case in the vast majority of instances when symbolic instruments come into play. A child who plays airplane, whatever else he does, does not challenge his operative knowing of airplanes but at best uses his habitual knowing of planes and applies it to a play situation. If a child tells his mother, "My finger is bleeding," the child's operative knowing concerning anatomy or blood vessels does not advance any more through the verbal expression than if he merely ran to the mother and cried pointing to the hurt. Socially and emotionally, such verbal exchange is of course valuable and desirable and may have all kinds of consequences. But these situations illustrate what I alluded to at the end of the last letter when I said that symbolic use does not by itself challenge operative structures. And when I continued and referred to the potential danger inherent in the egocentric figurative aspect of the symbol, I had in mind particularly the verbal language.

Precisely because of the almost infinite possibilities for constructive purposes, language can easily degenerate into an instrument that restricts healthy growth. This negative influence can become evident in the emotional area, an aspect to which I refer only in passing. It has been observed that deaf children grow up in an unaccepting environment. The milieu is strange to them as far as social communication is concerned and gives them to understand (mainly through the treatment of experts) that their acceptance as fully valued persons is conditional on their learning language. As I mentioned to you, they usually do not do well on this task. Thus I have long been surprised at the relative emotional health with which deaf youngsters grow up in a situation where the psychology of the hearing child could predict severe emotional risks. Is it possible that deaf children are spared the "risk" of early exposure to verbal situations? When hearing children for personal reasons cannot digest heard verbal expressions or fixate on egocentric meanings, such situations could easily contribute to later emotional instability.

But let us focus on the potential danger of dulling intellectual curiosity and strength by imposing a ready-made verbal language. It is said that through language society provides the infant with a powerful tool which it will take him many years to learn to use well. Is this not like presenting a three-year-old child with a 500-horsepower automobile? In this respect, language differs from other symbols. These other symbols, like images, customs, gestures, are in many ways more spontaneous to the child's personality and, in any case, cannot be easily manipulated by society. But language is presented as a ready-made system to the hearing child. There is always a certain danger that the system is imposed too powerfully and takes away from the child the spirit of initiative and discovery. However, I do not want to exaggerate these dangers. They are part of any human environment. The child's attachment to and assimilation of parental values, if imprudently imposed, can also have stultifying effects. Nor do I want to speak of the ordinary human tendency to substitute verbal habits for critical thinking. But I want to stress that real harm is done when linguistic patterns are imposed in early formal training, when linguistic behavior is held up as criterion of intellectual capacity at an age when language is still far behind the available capacity of operative thinking.

As you know, I speak here of the early school grades and their emphasis on linguistic skills, particularly those out-of-the-ordinary life skills of reading and writing. In grade one or two, it is very hard to make of reading and writing an activity that challenges the operative capacity of the child. In Piaget's terminology, early education emphasizes figurative—that is, low-level operative—knowing. When the child spontaneously engages in figurative knowing, as in ordinary conversation or in play, he does so for his own good reasons that stem from his personal needs and conditions. If he readily accepts the teaching and learning of figurative skills, again there is perhaps no psychological harm in that. But when reading is overemphasized and the child, for intellectual, social or emotional reasons, is not ready for it, then we should not be surprised at the number of intellectual and social failures we see around us.

I know that you, along with many teachers, have objected to my categorical statements that during early grades a simultaneous focus on reading and on challenging thinking is incompatible. In the interest of fairness and balance of arguments, I should state my case in a slightly different manner. Rather than saying that stressing reading is frequently harmful (a fact) and cannot but interfere with a healthy growth of intelligence (a hypothesis), let me be content to ask you to demonstrate that thinking can be furthered through reading exercises. In other words, in the past it has been unquestionably accepted that learning to read is good for intellectual growth. Now let the verdict be "not proven." If you know what challenging operative thinking is and you can devise linguistic or reading activities conducive to thinking, I have, of course, no objection to these activities. For example, as the child grows out of egocentric speech, linguistic play with phonemes and miscellaneous sounds, rhythms, and sing-song games help the child realize the basic arbitrariness of speech. Later, practice in verbal punning and joking is not only good exercise for vocabulary but also provides an opportunity for reflection on the relativity of semantics and the reversibility and decentration of meaning. Indeed, I have one colleague who insists that learning to make verbal puns and to carry on a joking repartee by remote word associations is the one linguistic activity that helps children to develop both verbal skill and logical and creative thinking.

In conclusion, we have made an effort in this letter to view the language of society within the framework of Piaget's theory of operative intelligence and symbol formation. We have stressed the similarities between linguistic and other symbolic behavior, in their acquisition, their use, and their dependence on operative structures. We attempted to show that the linguistic medium, as much as other symbolic media, contributes its share to keep thinking preoperational. When thinking structures approach the stage of formal operational intelligence, then and not earlier does the linguistic discourse become the proper medium through which to expand and apply operational thinking.

You told me once that critical reading of books is rare, even in a place like a graduate school, where you would most expect it. Now think of the early reading experiences of most American children. Did they take place in a setting where operative thinking was stressed and rewarded? Or was reading not rather a task where figurative skills were practiced, and was not the setting one that discouraged rather than encouraged thinking? It would be no exaggeration to say that schools still train our children to have their first reading experiences without concomitant thinking experiences. If we want our children to grow up so that they use the tremendous tool of speech and writing in a thinking manner, it is time to put the priorities according to the natural order of things: thinking first, then language.

I have used much language to say these things. I must give you time now for thinking. Please, give my best wishes to your colleagues.

Cordially yours,

motivation in learning and development

LETTER 7

Dear Teacher:

I know that you can hardly wait for practical, down-to-earth examples. As you read these pages and reluctantly (or willingly) admit that verbal language may not be the ideal medium for stimulating the thinking of your children in class, a growing impatience gets hold of you and your colleagues. If we do not teach these specific skills, what should we do? How can we fill up the hours of a school day with thinking activities? I will come to this in my very next letter because I realize that negative criticism alone is of no avail.

In the meantime, it is a pleasure to observe that many new ideas, already being put into the practice of education, point in the same direction as the one I am suggesting. But since my first aim is to clarify Piaget's concept of thinking, I must spend this one last letter on a topic that is strangely unfamiliar to psychology and even to education. I say "strangely" because it takes a mental tour de force to avoid the topic, as thoroughly as is being done in academic circles throughout the country.

Here is the point at issue. We all know, or at least we think that we know, what learning is. Learning is the acquisition of new knowledge. We do not offhand see a problem in this statement. What actually is the acquisition of new knowledge? Well, everybody knows that; it is learning!

Is this again an unfair question on my part? I could suggest that the acquisition of knowledge is not something that should be treated as cavalierly as the acquisition of a new shirt or a second car. But even granting that this point could be glossed over, what stance should we take regarding the growth of intelligence? Do we "learn" intelligence in a manner similar to the way in which we learn new knowledge? To this most behavioral scientists say yes. To this Piaget, and common sense, say no. (This time verbal habits are on our side. It does not make sense to say that one "learns intelligence.")

For Piaget the growth of intelligence is something quite different from the acquisition of new habits or new information. If the second is called learning, Piaget calls the first process development. These two psychological processes differ on at least five related points:

1. The experience from which they derive their sustenance
2. The motivation that provides energy for change
3. The memory that retains the new behavior over time
4. The type of knowing that is acquired
5. The mode in which the newly acquired behavior relates to previous behavior.

After we have discussed these five points with regard to development and to learning separately, we will conclude our summary of Piaget's theory by relating learning and development.

1. In order for the intelligence of a child to grow, he has to be active in a general human environment. For instance, a child acquires concepts of space and time by living in an environment in which he has to orient himself with regard to stable and changing objects occupying space. Further, he orients himself with regard to past and anticipated regularities and changes over time. Operational concepts of space and time are abstracted from practical coordinations in space and in time, rather than from things as such in the environment. This is a *formal abstraction* that abstracts the general form of a human activity. Piaget holds that the structures of operational intelligence derive by formal abstraction from the general coordinations of actions. He calls the source of these general concepts *general experience,* for the reason that it is common to all human beings.

In distinction from development, learning requires a *special experience.* To learn that the day is divided into 24 hours, a child must live in a specific environment that teaches him this division. To learn the names for the temporal divisions requires a certain linguistic environment; to learn what a subway is requires specific encounters that are limited to certain human individuals, and so on. Consequently, the source of things that are learned is in part the figuratively present physical (real) or social (including symbolic) environment. Things that are learned can also be considered as abstracted. Whereas development proceeds by formal abstraction, learning takes place by way of *physical abstraction;* that is, the child learns to focus on relevant and to disregard less relevant attributes and to recognize, say, a subway, even if it is presented in many different ways.

2. The prime motivation for intellectual development comes from within the operative structure. A child's intelligence develops because it functions. Developing and functioning are the same process for the operative structures. The rules internal to the functioning are the same as those that characterize the development. If functioning is considered as resulting from an equilibration between assimilation and accommodation, development too is seen as resulting from an equilibration between the various contributing forces in the environment.

This view has rather important practical consequences. It means that intellectual development is the birthright of every human being and actually takes place in any environment. It also means that parents and educators need not frantically look for contrived situations or rewards that will make intelligence grow. Intelligence grows from *within.* Thus the task becomes one of furthering and nourishing this growth by providing suitable opportunities, not by explicit teaching of what to do or what to know.

Learning, however, is a different matter; it usually depends very much upon some reward or reason that lies outside the learning process. On this score many of the so-called learning strategies and schedules are well taken. Under ordinary circumstances a child who is shown some memorizing strategies and is promised an ice-cream cone will learn the names of the presidents of the United States sooner and better than a child who does not have these outside helps.

3. There is no need to postulate a memory factor for operative structures. Memory for operative structures is in their functioning. Nobody need *remember* that a subclass is included in a superior class or that the reverse drawing of P is ꟼ . Once these things are

known, they are available; if a child "forgets" them, this only proves that he has never known them.

With learning, however, forgetting is never far away. A friend of mine with whom I spoke not long ago lived for three years in Oregon and could not recall the number of the house or the name of the street where he lived. He could not even recognize a picture of the house. What does this mean? It says something about the weakness of his figurative knowing, but in spite of that I am not worried at all about his operative intelligence.

4. Although intelligence can be referred to as knowing, it is better to view it as a general instrument of knowing. It is not concerned with particulars, but provides the framework (forms) within which any particular knowing takes place. Thus intelligence deals with general concepts, such as the object concept—to regard things as separate, existing objects—the class concept, the relation concept, the concepts of logical reasoning, and so forth.

Learning, on the other hand, properly deals with particular knowledge and new information. The results of learning give us the contents of all the things we know, from soup to nuts, in all their various forms: knowledge of physical things, of persons, of verbal expressions, of content of books, and so on.

5. Intellectual development, strictly speaking, cannot go wrong. Later structures build upon earlier structures and incorporate them in a higher synthesis. Sensorimotor coordinations do not disappear with operational spatial concepts. Moreover, with increasing development knowing takes on the character of being necessary and universal, that is, independent of particular circumstances. It converges on but a single logic, though expression and use of that logic will necessarily take many diverse forms. It therefore provides the firm basis on which truth and critical evidence can rest.

The results of learning, however, are always subject to error. I learned in school that the human cell had 24 chromosome pairs; now we are told there are only 23 pairs. Here one information is substituted for another. I learn that daylight saving time is used in one place and not in another. All these particular knowledges are contingent upon particular circumstances and can never be as self-evident as the forms of the operational structures.

So far I have sketched for you five major differences between development and learning. In real life, however, these processes go hand in hand, and we must try to clarify the relations between them.

To say it succinctly, the developed structures constitute the basic capacity which makes particular learning possible. Or, to express it in another way, the available structures determine the manner in which particular knowledge is assimilated. The relation between learning and development is therefore a relation of content to form, analogous to other relations we have touched upon, such as the relation of functioning to structure and the relation of figurative to operative knowing.

Take as an example the learning of the statement, "Paris is the capital city of France." It would not be difficult to teach this verbal expression to a three-year-old child. He could learn to respond with "Paris" to the question: "What is the name of the capital city of France?" An eight-year-old child and a 13-year-old child are likewise taught the same statement. Since in Piaget's theory acquisition of all knowledge means assimilation of new knowledge to available structures, let us ask what are the typical knowing structures to which the learning of the name is assimilated. It is then perfectly clear that the learning of these three children will differ foremost as a function of their developed general structures. Of course, this opinion does not deny that additional factors may differentially influence the understanding of the three children. To the three-year-old child, the question is assimilated to such problems as "What's the name of your friend?" and "What's the name of this?" (pointing to his hair). The child has no capacity to understand what a city or a country is; he does not know the relation between the name and the city. If you doubt this, ask a four-year-old child who lives in Ottawa what came first, the city or the river, or ask him whether his friend Tom could be called Tim.

A seven-year-old child who also learns the name "Paris" has more advanced knowing schemes to which to assimilate the problem, but even for him the nature of a country and its relation to a city and the function of government and of a capital city are quite vague and undetermined. He does not have the spatial, temporal, or social perspectives to put the new information on a firm operative basis. For him, even more than for the three-year-old child, such a knowing is figurative and low-level operative: that is, he knows some verbal configurations about a place (the particular name), but he does not understand the nature of the place and its relation to other places. This knowing, if it is unduly stressed, can be intellectually harmful precisely because the child is quite capable of *some* operational understanding about place, time, and society. Instead, he is taught a descriptive name about things and cannot at the same time engage his full operative skill toward them. He learns to talk by rote, when this should be discouraged and he should be encouraged to talk with understanding.

A 13-year-old child in our society commonly has developed adequate operative schemes so that he can assimilate the new name of a capital city to a general knowledge of geography and history. Only then is it at all possible that the child may have a spontaneous intellectual curiosity to remember the name, whereas in the younger child the learning of that name would require strong extrinsic motivation.

On this point I recall an interesting story. My neighbor's son Ted is a big, curious lad who frequently visits our home. One day, when he was still four years old, I said to him, "How much is two plus three?" He looked at me and asked, "What is *plus?*" I replied that plus means "and, together." "Oh," he said, "two and three together make five." Next day I asked, "How much is three plus three?" He looked at me and asked, "What does *plus* mean?" I explained and forthwith obtained the correct answer. Thereafter, I asked once more with plus, got the familiar question, explained, and then obtained the right reply. This went on for some time until one day for some reason he no longer asked what plus meant. By that time he had mastered the notion that the particular order made no difference, that 4 plus 2 is the same as 2 plus 4. Some months later I asked, "How much is four minus three? Ted looked at me and asked, "What does *minus* mean?" I replied, "Minus means less, take away." Ted with some hesitation reacted by saying, "One." The day after I asked again, "How much is three minus two?" Again Ted's question about minus, my reply, and Ted's final answer. This also went on for some weeks until about the time that he comprehended that if 2 plus 3 equals 5, then 5 minus 3 equals 2. At that time he accepted the word "minus."

About a year later I started asking him questions about multiplying: "How much is two times three?" To which Ted said, "What does *times* mean?" My reply: "You take it three times, two and two and two." Here also the same questioning was repeated for some time until Ted fairly well demonstrated the knowledge that three times five is the same as five times three.

I recall now that at the time I felt some slight annoyance at the child's unwillingness to learn one little name, particularly since he was obviously a bright child and on other occasions remembered names of friends or places which he only encountered once. When, some months after the last incident, I started questioning about division and he came up with his familiar, "What does *divide* mean?" it suddenly occurred to me that the child was exemplifying the salutary motto: thinking first, then language. He showed a healthy resistance to burdening his mind with figurative names, the meanings of which were vague to him. But as soon as he began to have some operative understanding of the number system, he was quite willing to attach arbitrary labels to specific, meaningful operations.

This child's behavior is an obvious example of why the distinction between development and learning is much more than an academic exercise. It goes to the very heart of the teaching process. If this child had been in a setting where recall of the particular words was overemphasized, he may quite likely have turned against the operative skill. Being left to his own tempo, he was at first unwilling to learn strange words, but enjoyed and progressed along operative skills. His intellect developed, and once it had reached a certain stage, he learned and painlessly remembered the words that now represented something meaningful, namely, some activity into which he could put his intellectual teeth. Before that, these words would have been descriptive names, referring to a figurative knowing, the meaning of which he had to make a special effort not to forget.

I grant you that many teachers intuitively know the difference between development and learning. Moreover, does not their training deal at great length with the topics of maturation and readiness? Leaving semantic differences aside, what do maturation and readiness really imply? Maturation implies a physiological development, such as faster nerve conduction, stronger muscles, finer sensory focusing. Readiness, on the other hand, means a prior learning of skills that are supposed to be necessary before one can learn a new skill. In other words, prior physiological development or prior psychological learning experience exhausts the scope covered by these two concepts. But operative development, with which we are dealing here, is neither readiness nor maturation. It is not a physiological process or an accumulation of learning experiences. It cannot do without these; that is, it needs a healthy organism and specific learning experiences. But learning takes place through a process which in its functioning is different from intellectual growth and is experienced as being different by the knowing subject.

In their extreme forms, the differences between learning and development are striking and obvious to everybody. But if one analyzes knowing into figurative and operative aspects, one is able to point out the different contributions attributable to development or to learning even in more complex situations. As a rule, figurative aspects are related to learning, whereas operative aspects of the knowing situation invariably point to development.

In fact, why do I have you make a laborious mental analysis of operative and figurative knowing and distinguish between figurative and operative aspects of a symbol, including verbal behavior? It is to put you in a position to pay attention to the developmental contribution in a learning situation. For how could you nourish and use the motivation intrinsic to development unless you had confidence that such motivation is present? Further, I want you to become sensitive to its manifestation.

If you grasp Piaget's biological perspective of intelligence, you will never be able to say what a young teacher said to me about her first graders: "But they can't think." These youngsters may not be able to speak properly or to read or to write; they may be poor in remembering or learning things by rote. But there is one thing they do, and must do, because they are children. This one thing is thinking. Six-year-old children develop. They are becoming more intelligent right under the nose of the teacher. This could not happen if they could not think. That they develop poorly in spite of schooling, instead of being helped by it, is the tragedy to which we address ourselves. This is the immediate reason that motivates me to urge all teachers to become familiar with Piaget's theory of knowledge.

Einstein worked out his theoretical formulation far from any practical application. Today no living person in unaffected in his daily life or in his moral stance by the practical results of these theories. Piaget was not primarily interested in education—or, for that matter, in psychology. But he did focus and work indefatigably on the problem of knowing as no man ever did before him. He became a great psychologist and a great educator almost as a by-product of his principal philosophical interest.

One problem that fascinated him, as it did others who considered theoretical knowledge, can be formulated in this way. If intelligent knowing is not a copy of reality, and if it does not derive primarily from the environment, how does it happen that it so perfectly fits the environment? Why is it that theoretical abstractions such as numbers and deductive reasoning have such fruitful applications in the real world?

To this Piaget suggests a biological answer, which puts him in opposition to current scientific and philosophical opinions. He denies that the general instruments of knowing, the forms of human intelligence, are discovered or learned from the environment. He denies with equal vigor that these forms are innately given or belong to a supranatural realm. He holds that human intelligence derives from the functioning of its inner structures according to a process of equilibration by way of formal abstractions. But the functioning of these structures does not take place in a vacuum. It occurs within a concrete person who lives in a specific physical and social environment, from which he learns specific things and toward which he has personal attitudes and motivation. The functioning of the structures manifests in behavior (and eventually to subjective awareness) the "objective" regulations that are internal to the functioning of all things in nature. Human intelligence is, therefore, directly related to regulations that can be observed at various levels of natural functioning.

If Piaget suggests that development is "natural" to knowledge, all this may sound very theoretical or philosophical. But if educators would take this statement seriously and look carefully for its behavioral manifestations, who knows how many megatons of intellectual energy could be freed for a society that is desperately in need of new perspectives?

A linguist once listened to a colloquium in which the lecturer pointed out the well-documented proclivity for engaging in linguistic habits with a minimum of operative thinking. This is an example of what is commonly called the influence of language on thinking, when in reality it should be referred to as the abdication of thinking in favor of linguistic habits. The lecturer continued by suggesting that formal education should, right from the beginning, train against this habit instead of unwittingly reinforcing it. To this the linguist exclaimed, "But do you know what would happen to us if all schools suddenly adopted your program? It would altogether change the use of language and social life with it." Perhaps it would. However, the likelihood of any quick and massive change in educational procedures is really quite remote. But that Piaget's theory, like all great theories, is eminently practical and, if practiced, will have revolutionary effects, I do not doubt.

The next letters will provide you with long overdue examples of how operative thinking can be brought into the classroom. If you still find Piaget's position somewhat theoretical and irrelevant, it is high time we turned to down-to-earth applications. Thank you for the hard work you have done so far.

Sincerely yours,

schools
for
thinking

PART TWO

symbol-
picture
logic

LETTER 8

Dear Teacher:

This letter is prepared to make you an active participant in the thinking exercises. If you like, cover the right-hand side of the following pages and construct your own answers before you check for an appropriate response to a given problem. Remember, however, that in a classroom situation these exercises proceed in open group form and in a flexible give-and-take fashion. Children come to the board to solve a problem, sometimes also to pose a problem. There are spontaneous additions, erasures, and corrections that cannot be easily reproduced here.

This is how the exercise starts. You first see an example and then you continue according to the given demonstration.

Example: $H \longrightarrow$

Now continue by substituting something in place of the ?

? $\longrightarrow$		S
? $\longrightarrow$		T
? $\longrightarrow$		A

These four categories are the basic universe to which we limit our examples. Appropriate responses are provided in the margin. Note that generally other alternative responses

85

are acceptable. The ones in the margin are only usual answers which a child can be expected to give in response to the question. The exercises are grouped progressively into seven parts. Depending on the capacity of the children, one may spend part of a period or several periods on each section. Constant review of covered material is of course in order. From my own experience I can hazard the guess that the proposed exercises suffice for a symbol logic course, two periods a week, throughout a school year in grades three to five.

In the following demonstration an asterisk (*) on the left-hand side of the page indicates that an alternative response, different from one before, is required. (Ex.) stands for example. On the blackboard we do not actually write the ?, but leave a blank. We then make clear to the children that the blank has to be filled in. In some cases we request a specific number or combination of symbols or things. Such a request is also indicated in the following exercise by means of a ?, as you will see.

Remember that in class we do not verbalize explicit meanings of the symbolic expressions to the children. We let them discover the exact logical meaning by repeated demonstrations and by setting specific problems according to individual need. You may therefore find the following demonstrations rather difficult and feel that you are left in the dark unnecessarily. This is, of course, partly because there is no real person to respond to your specific queries. In addition, I provide here simply an overview without a sufficient number of exercises and reviews. And, if you prefer, you can turn first to the end of the letter where I explain the meaning of each symbolic expression. My experience shows that children, given adequate time and practice, have no particular difficulty with this method but, on the contrary, enjoy the opportunity to make their own discoveries.

PART 1   The basic elements

(Ex.) S ⟶ ☼

      H ⟶ ? ; T ⟶ ?   ⌂, ♀

(Ex.) H ⟶ { ⌂ ♀ / ♀ ⌂ / ⌂ ⌂ }   (Example)

(Correct the following:)

               (Substitute something for ?)
    H ⟶ ♀ ☼ ?   ⌂

    ? ⟶ } (Substitute something for ?) A
           ⊂ ⌂
* ? ⟶ (Substitute an alternative) H

    ? ⟶ }   T
          ♀ ☼ ♀
* ? ⟶   S

    ? ⟶ ⊂   A

    ? ⟶ ⊂ ⊂   A

    ? ⟶ ⊂ ⊂ ⊂   A

(Ex.) T ⇸ ⊂   (⇸ is a new symbol)

        (?   ♀   ⟶
        { ?   ♀ ☼   ⟶
T   { ?   ☼ ⌂   ⇸
        (?   ☼ ⌂ ♀   ⟶

87

A → ?

A → { ? / ? * / ? *

(Remember that the responses shown in the margin are only possible correct responses. There is never only one correct response except in the case of the arrows [→, ↛] where one of the alternatives is definitely correct and the other is false.)

? → { ☼
? ↛

* ? ↛   ☼ ⌂

(Correct the following:) H → ⌀

(One way:) ?

(Another way:) ?

? →
* ? →
? ↛   ⌀ ♀
* ? ↛

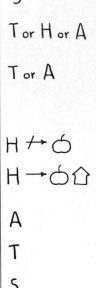

S

T or H or A

T or A

H ↛ ⌀

H → ⌀ ⌂

A

T

S

H

A ⟶ ?

(Ex.) Ā ⟶ { 🌳 🏠 ☀ }   (⁻ is a new symbol)

? ⟶
* ? ⟶   } 🍎
* ? ⟶
* ? ⟶

H ⟶ ?

H { ↛ ?
    ↛ ? *
    ↛ ? * }

H̄ ⟶ ? ?   (Two things)

H̄ ⟶ ? ☀ 🌳 🏠

? ⟶
* ? ⟶   } ☀
* ? ↛
* ? ↛

🍎

A
H̄
T̄
S̄
🏠
🌳
☀
🍎
☀ 🌳
↛
S
T̄
H̄
Ā

$\overline{A}$ { → ? (One thing)   🏠 or 🎈 or ☀

    ↛ ?   🍎

$\overline{S}$ ↛ ? ? (Two things)   ☀🍎 or ☀🏠

                     or ☀🎈

$\overline{H}$ ↛ ? (One thing)   🏠

$\overline{?}$ ↛ 🎈   T

$\overline{?}$ ↛ ☀ 🏠   S or H

PART 3 Conjunction

H → ?   🏠

T → ?   🎈

H ? 🎈 🏠   →

T ? 🎈 🏠   →

(Ex.) T • H {
     → 🎈 🏠
     → 🏠 🎈   (• is a new
     ↛ 🎈   symbol)
     ↛ 🏠

S • A → ?   ☀ 🍎

A • S → ?   ☀ 🍎

A • S → ?   *   🍎 ☀

90

Left	Arrow	Note	Answer
? • ?	→	(Two symbols)	S·A
?	→	(One symbol)	S
* ?	→	(Continue with one symbol)	A
* ?	→	☼ ○	H̄
* ?	→		T̄
?	⊬		T
* ?	⊬		H

Left		Note	Answer
T · H	?	☼ ○	⊬
S̄	?		⊬
Ā	?		⊬

H · A
Arrow				Answer
→	?			⇧ ○
⊬	?	?	(Continue with two things)	☼ ♀
⊬	?	?	*	☼ ○
⊬	?	?	*	⇧ ♀

Left				Answer
T · S	?	⇧ ☼		⊬
H · T	?	⇧ ☼		⊬
H	?	♀ ⇧		→
H · T	?	⇧		⊬

(Correct this expression without erasing any part) S · T → ☼

		Answer
(One way:)	?	S·T ⊬ ☼
(Another way:)	?	S·T → ☼♀

A · H ?   } ↦
A ?   } 🏠 🌳   ↦
H ?   }   →

PART 4 Negation Within Conjunction

(Ex.) H · T̄
{
→ 🏠 ☀
→ 🏠 🍎
→ 🏠
↦ ☀
}

Ā · S
{
→ ? ? (Two things)   🏠 ☀
→ ? ? *   🍄 ☀
→ ? (One thing)   ☀
↦ ?   🍄 or 🏠 or 🍎
}

T → ?   🍄

(Ex.) T̄
{
→ ?   ☀
→ ?   🏠
→ ∅   (Here, Nothing ∅ is a new "thing")
}

H̄ · T
{
→ ? ?   ☀ 🍄
→ ? ? *   🍄 🍎
→ ?   🍄
}

H̄ · T ? ∅   ↦

$?\ \longrightarrow$ H

$?\bullet? \longrightarrow$ $H\cdot\bar{T}$

* $?\bullet? \longrightarrow$ $H\cdot\bar{A}$ or $H\cdot\bar{S}$

$\bar{?}\bullet\bar{?} \longrightarrow$ $\bar{A}\cdot\bar{T}$

* $\bar{?}\bullet\bar{?} \longrightarrow$ $\bar{A}\cdot\bar{S}$

$\bar{T} \longrightarrow$ $\longrightarrow$

$\bar{A}\cdot\bar{S}$

$\longrightarrow ?$ (One thing)

$\longrightarrow ?$ *

$\longrightarrow ?\quad ?$ (Two things)

$?\quad\emptyset$

$?\ \bigcirc$

$?\ \bigcirc\ \bigtriangleup$

$\bar{H}\quad ?$

$H\quad ?$ $\emptyset$

$\bar{H}\cdot T\quad ?$

$\bar{H}\cdot\bar{T}\quad ?$

$A\cdot H\quad ?$

$?\ \longrightarrow$ (One symbol) A or H

* $?\ \longrightarrow$ (One symbol) $\bar{S}$ or $\bar{T}$

93

? • ? →			T·S or S·T
* ? • ? →			$\overline{H}$·S, T·$\overline{A}$, $\overline{H}$·T
* ? • ? →			$\overline{H}$·$\overline{A}$ or $\overline{A}$·S
? →			T or S
? +→			H or A
* ? +→	♀ ☼		$\overline{T}$ or $\overline{S}$
T · H ?			+→
T · A			+→
T · $\overline{A}$?			→
$\overline{T}$ · A ?			+→
$\overline{T}$ · $\overline{A}$?			+→

?	∅		+→
$\overline{T}$ · A →	?	(One thing)	◌
+→	?	(One thing)	⌂ or ☼

?	∅		+→
→	?	(One thing)	◌
$\overline{T}$ · A { ?	♀		+→
?	⌂		+→
?	◌		→

94

Before we continue with Part 5 let us take a breather. I hope you see what we are driving at. I am sure you have some urgent questions. Perhaps you know symbolic logic and object to some of the ways in which I am using symbols. Remember that I am not primarily interested in teaching a specific symbol logic, not even "logic" as such. In this connection I recall that Piaget's logical formulations have been criticized as not being sufficiently elegant—to which he replied that he had set out not to compose a logical system but to observe the child's spontaneously developing logic.

Consider what may be going on as the child solves the given problems. Evaluate the procedure in terms of the challenge to the child's operative intelligence, not primarily in terms of what it means to an adult or to one trained in logic and mathematics.

PART 5 Negated Conjunction

(Ex.) $H \longrightarrow$ 🏠 , $\overline{H} \longrightarrow \emptyset$

(Ex.) $H \cdot T \longrightarrow$ 🏠 🌳

$$\overline{H} \cdot \overline{T} \begin{cases} ? & \emptyset & \longrightarrow \\ ? & \text{🏠} & \longmapsto \\ ? & \text{🍎 🌳} & \longmapsto \end{cases}$$

$$H \cdot T \begin{cases} ? & \text{🍎 🌳} & \longmapsto \\ ? & \text{🏠 ☀} & \longmapsto \\ ? & \text{🌳} & \longmapsto \\ ? & \text{🏠 🌳} & \longrightarrow \end{cases}$$

$$\text{(Ex.) } H \mathbin{\overline{\cdot}} T \begin{cases} \longrightarrow & \text{🍎 🌳} \\ \longrightarrow & \text{🏠 ☀} \\ \longrightarrow & \text{🌳} \\ \longmapsto & \text{🏠 🌳} \end{cases}$$

($\overline{\cdot}$ is a new combination)

$A \cdot S \quad ?$ $\left.\begin{matrix} \\ \\ \\ \end{matrix}\right\}$ 🍎 $\qquad \longmapsto$

$\overline{A} \cdot \overline{S} \quad ?$ $\qquad \longmapsto$

$A \mathbin{\overline{\cdot}} S \quad ?$ $\qquad \longrightarrow$

$T \cdot A \quad \longmapsto \quad ?$ $\qquad$ (One thing) $\quad|\quad$ Any <u>one</u> thing

$T \cdot A \quad ? \quad \emptyset$ $\qquad \longmapsto$

$$T \mathbin{\overline{\cdot}} A \begin{cases} ? & \text{🏠} & \longrightarrow \\ ? & \text{🌳} & \longrightarrow \\ ? & \emptyset & \longrightarrow \end{cases}$$

$S \mathbin{\overline{\cdot}} H$?
$S \mathbin{\overline{\cdot}} H$?
$\overline{S} \cdot \overline{H}$?
$\overline{S}$?
$\overline{H}$?

} ☀

↛
→
↛
↛
→

$S \cdot H$?
$S \mathbin{\overline{\cdot}} H$?
$\overline{S} \cdot \overline{H}$?
$\overline{S}$?
$\overline{H}$

} 🌳

↛
→
→
→
→

PART 6 Disjunction

(Ex.) $T \cdot H$
{
→ 🌳 🏠
↛ 🌳
↛ 🏠 ☀
↛ 🍎 ☀
}

(Ex.) $T \vee H$
{
→ 🌳 🏠 (v is a new symbol)
→ 🌳
→ 🏠 ☀
→ ☀
}

$S \vee H$?
$S \cdot H$?

} ☀ 🍎

→
↛

97

S · A ? } 🍎   ↦

S ∨ A ?   →

H̄ · S ? } ☀   →

H̄ ∨ S ?   →

H̄ · S ? } ⌂ ☀   ↦

H̄ ∨ S ?   →

T · Ā ? } ∅   ↦

T ∨ Ā ?   →

Ā ∨ H̄ ? } 🌳 ☀   →

Ā · H̄ ?   →

Ā ∨ H̄ ? } 🍎 ☀   →

Ā · H̄ ?   ↦

          ? 🌳   →

Ā ∨ H̄   ? 🍎   →

          ? ⌂   →

(Ex.) Ā ∨ H̄   ↦

                 →

Ā · H̄   ? 🍎   ↦

         ? ⌂   ↦

(Disjunction with
Negation is new)

(Ex.) $\overline{A} \cdot \overline{H}$ ↛ 🍎 🏠 $\begin{cases} \overline{T} \vee \overline{H}, \text{ or} \\ \overline{T} \vee \overline{S}, \text{ or} \\ \overline{T} \vee \overline{A} \end{cases}$

     $\overline{?} \vee \overline{?}$ → 🏠 ☀ 🍎

     $\overline{?} \vee \overline{?}$ ↛ 🏠 ☀ $\overline{H} \vee \overline{S}$

     $? \vee ?$ ↛ 🏠 ☀ $T \vee A$

PART 7 Negated Disjunction

(Ex.) $A \overset{\cdot}{\vee} H$ → 🍎

(Ex.) $A \overline{\vee} H$ ↛ 🍎   ($\overline{\vee}$ is new)

(Ex.) $\overline{A} \cdot \overline{H}$ ↛ 🍎

(Ex.) $A \overline{\vee} H$ → 🌳

(Ex.) $A \overline{\vee} H$ ↛ 🏠

$\overline{T} \vee S$?   ↛

$T \vee \overline{S}$?   →

$\overline{T} \vee \overline{S}$? $\Bigg\}$ 🌳 🏠   →

$T \vee S$?   →

$T \overline{\vee} S$?   ↛

		(One symbol)	H or S
			$\overline{T}$ or $\overline{A}$
? • ?		(Two symbols)	H · S
$\overline{?}$ • ?			$\overline{T}$·S or $\overline{T}$·H or $\overline{A}$·S or $\overline{A}$·H
$\overline{?}$ • $\overline{?}$			$\overline{A}$ · $\overline{T}$
H ∓ ?			T or A
? ∨ T			S or H
$\overline{?}$ ∨ A			$\overline{T}$
$\overline{S}$ ∨ $\overline{?}$			$\overline{T}$ or $\overline{A}$
? ∨̲ ?			T ∨̲ A

(Ex.) $\overline{H}$ • $\overline{T}$ ↛ 🏠 🌳

H ∨̲ T ↛ ?   🏠 ⚲

(Ex.) $\overline{H}$ ∨ $\overline{T}$ ↛ 🏠 🌳

H ∓ T ↛ ?   🏠 ⚲

$\overline{H}$ • $\overline{T}$ → ?   🍎 ☼ ∅

H ∨̲ T → ?   🍎 ☼ ∅

$\overline{H}$ • $\overline{T}$?   ↦   🏠 ⚲

H ∨̲ T ?   ↦   🏠 ⚲

$\overline{H}$ ∨ $\overline{T}$ → ? (One thing) Any one thing

H ∓ T → ? (One thing) Any one thing

$\overline{H}$ ∨ $\overline{T}$ ↛ ?   🏠 ⚲

H ∓ T ↛ ?   🏠 ⚲

This is about as far as we have gone up to grades four to six. We will now summarize the rationale behind the procedure in some detail.

First you notice that in all cases a problem consists of three parts. Generally, one of the parts has to be completed. On the left there is a symbolic expression, on the right the picture of a real thing and between these two an arrow or a crossed arrow indicating that the picture is or is not an appropriate instance of the symbolic expression. The symbols are arbitrary. But we have selected the first letters of the appropriate English words for the things and traditional symbols (⌐,•,v) for the logical connectives of negation, conjunction, and disjunction. We could have chosen other signs; we actually have done so without much difficulty. But since the purpose of the exercise is not memory, we minimized this particular aspect by using familiar letters. A symbol expresses a concept, a mental construct. *H* stands for the *class of houses* or for the proposition *"There is a house."*

Part 1 demonstrated a number of basic conceptual skills. First is the important difference between the *mental* symbolized concept and the *real* physical instance. The symbolic affirmation *H* is appropriate as long as there is a house in the picture. Anything else added to one house, such as other things or other houses, leaves the logical truth of the symbolic affirmation unaffected. Second, the children can see right from the start that there are many different instances of a symbolized concept, just as a real thing can be symbolized from different conceptual viewpoints. Every time you see an asterisk the child is urged to come up with an alternative response. Notice further that incorrect statements are put on the board (*H* → ⟳) and that children are given the opportunity to make corrections, and again there is more than one way to do this. Finally, children are shown that it is just as important to know what a concept or a thing is (→) as to know what it is not (↛).

Part 2 introduces the negation sign (⌐). Affirmation requires the presence, negation the absence of the thing symbolized. Negation opens up unlimited possibilities for symbolic variations. The combination of (negation) and (↛) leads to double negation, where one neutralizes the other ("The *negation* of a house—is *not*—a house").

Part 3 demonstrates the conjunctive combination (•), e.g., H•A means that *both* a house *and* an apple must be present. In the affirmative case, the conjunction requires the *combined presence* of instances belonging to both elements of the symbolic expression.

In this particular procedure a child has to comprehend that
$H \longrightarrow \bigcirc \; \bigtriangleup$, but $H \bullet A \nrightarrow \bigtriangleup$
This comprehension is not easily verbalized. In our ordinary con-
versation, we do not distinguish between a concept and an instance.
When we point to a table and say, "This is a table," we really imply
the following more correct expression: "This thing is *an instance* of
a table." You can verify for yourself that much confusion is generated
by our somewhat ambiguous verbal expressions. Everybody knows
that one of the reasons for inventing logical symbols was to clarify
these potential pitfalls created by everyday language. In fact, children's thinking is severely challenged by our procedure, which
clearly separates instance and symbolized concept. We have frequently observed this challenge in the children's manifest behavior.

Part 4 shows negated classes within the conjunction, and for the
first time makes unambiguously clear that in our procedure *negation
requires neither more nor less than the absence of the negated thing;*
hence O or nothing (the empty class) is appropriate as a real instance.
Part 5 introduces the negation sign over the conjunctive sign. You are
quite right that instead of $H \; \overline{\bullet} \; T$, we could have written — $(H \bullet T)$.
Children are here trained to comprehend the critical difference be-
tween $\overline{H} \bullet \overline{T}$ and $H \; \overline{\bullet} \; T$. This also is a case where ordinary language
falls down: "A house and a tree are absent" versus "It is not the case
that there is the combination of a house and a tree." Without explic-
itly saying so, we demonstrated that logically ($H \; \overline{\bullet} \; T \longrightarrow$) equals
$(H \bullet T \nrightarrow)$. We do not say this, for we want the children to *comprehend* a symbolic strategy rather than routinely *learn* figurative
rules. In traditional logic there is the danger that learning of symbolic
rules comes first and comprehension lags behind. In our case we are
effectively avoiding this danger by working with instances that cannot be manipulated as symbolic expressions. A child cannot pull out
a formula and get the right answer. For all that, I do not wish to imply
that use of habitual rules is harmful. Quite the opposite: it is psychologically desirable and appropriate and has its necessary place in
ordinary behavior. But symbolic manipulation should not be regarded as necessarily identical with operative thinking, and it is this
latter in which we are here primarily interested.

Parts 6 and 7, finally, illustrate the concept of inclusive disjunction
(v). This connective means "or" in the sense of "either one or the
other or both." We can also verbalize it as "At least one of the alternatives must be verified." When the alternatives include a negated

class, the absence of that class instance suffices, so that $\overline{H}$ v S
$\mathbb{Q}$. For your own understanding I point out that $(\overline{H} \bullet \overline{S})$ equals $(H\overline{v} \overline{S})$ and $(\overline{H}v \overline{S})$ equals $(H \mathbin{\overline{v}} S)$. When I say "equals" I mean that the two expressions are logically equivalent: all true or false instances of one expression are equally true or false instances of the other expression. The expressions are two ways of saying the same thing.

If a youngster masters the symbolic demonstrations we have presented thus far, what next? Can we continue and propose harder exercises? First of all, it is, of course, possible to continue and introduce more connectives, such as the implication sign $\supset$ ("if . . . then.") $H \supset T$ would stand for: "If a house is present, there must also be a tree present." $H \supset \overline{T}$, in similar fashion, would require the absence of a tree if a house is present. The critical test of implication is to ask for a false instance, e.g., $H \supset \overline{T} \nrightarrow$? The response to this question must include the combination of a house and a tree ($\bigtriangleup\mathbb{Q}$). The mere presence of a tree (e.g., $\dot{\bigcirc}$ $\mathbb{Q}$) does not falsify the expression $H \supset \overline{T}$.

We have attempted successfully the introduction of logical proofs or verbal logic, that is, using a verbal statement in connection with our "picture" statements. For instance, the teacher says, "It is false that there is a house but no tree." The children write: $H \bullet \overline{T} \nrightarrow$ and then fill in instances. An inventive teacher can employ all kinds of modifications. She can use shapes and colors and thus render a combination more realistic: $H \bullet B$ mean something that is both a house and blue; T v R would mean something that is either a tree or not red, and so on. We have also used a different system of presenting symbols and instances, which demonstrates more clearly the logical truth of each element in a combination.

The last thing I want you to think is that this demonstration or those you will read in other letters are fixed guidelines that should be followed to the letter. Consider them as exercises for the child's operative muscles. If children get bored because the exercises are too easy, I would think that they are in good shape to tackle the more difficult "verbal" logic. Let me explain. If a child can master the last exercises, he appears ready to apply his intellect to verbal material. He should be able to exercise his operative skills in reading and writing and to recognize the logical structures and reasoning that are implicit in the written material. This, after all, is the purpose of primary education: To nourish the growing intellect so that it is capable of handling the content of the various subjects presented in the advanced grades.

Sincerely yours,

other thinking games

Dear Teacher:

You ask me how the symbol-picture logic presented in the last letter differs from traditional logic. Does our system have an advantage over the logic taught in college? I would say that the two systems serve different purposes. Our system is suitable for children of primary-school age; traditional deductive logic serves adults. Our purpose is to exercise the thinking of these children, not to teach a system, whereas the purpose of traditional logic is precisely to construct a well-formulated system. Our focus is not the system but the concrete operational child, who functions well when his concepts are applied to concrete events. Thus our method constantly matches a symbol-conceptual expression with "real" instances (in pictures) in accordance with the young child's natural bent. Traditional logic, like algebra, deals primarily with symbol-conceptual expressions throughout and therefore suits a later period in conceptual development, which Piaget designates as formal operational.

Moreover, there is a danger in the use of any system of symbols. A person can memorize rules, but these rules may not engage fully the intellectual structures of the one who uses the symbolic rules. A child can learn logical or algebraic formulas by rote and can thus rearrange symbols. This, however, is not a thinking but, at best, a memory exercise. We do not want our children merely to remember that $H \bar{v} B$ can be verbalized as "anything that does not contain H or B"; we want children to comprehend the concept of the negation of a disjunction. This comprehension implies an active assimilation of the symbolic expression to a structure of knowing which the child has available and strengthens through actual use.

I should have mentioned that we have used our logic successfully in ordinary grade-school classes over quite extensive periods. We have also used it in special classes with deaf children and with children on the Navaho reservation who, like deaf children, have great difficulties with the English language. When one observes linguistically and scholastically poor children performing well on thinking tasks such as our symbol-picture logic, or other thinking tasks which I will describe presently, one cannot help being deeply impressed with the basically nonlinguistic nature of human intelligence. I recall the 13-year-old deaf child who was in school for the first time at that age and thus knew practically no English or any other social language. When this lad realized that a thing, such as a yellow tree, can be symbolized in many different ways ($\mapsto T \cdot Y, T \cdot \bar{B}, \bar{H} \cdot \bar{W}, S \vee Y, \bar{T} \vee Y, \bar{B}, T \bar{\bullet} B, T \vee Y$, etc., or $\mapsto H \cdot Y, \bar{T}, H \vee \bar{Y}$, etc., etc.) he became so excited that he ran out of the room to communicate this discovery to other teachers. Or I think of the teachers who spend most of the time drilling fixed connectives into the children's mind; how astonished they were when they observed these children in the logic class actively correcting mistakes which I, the teacher, failed to notice.

I wholeheartedly agree with your remarks that all good teaching focuses on the thinking component of a task that has to be learned. In particular, a good remedial teacher will invariably make the task challenging and in this way engage the child's intrinsic motivation. A primary focus on the intelligent use of the senses and the muscles is found today in the perceptual and motor training methods used in many schools and clinics, and in the visual training methods employed by optometrists in cases of visual dysfunction. But why should we wait until the child is beginning to be seriously deficient in performance and to experience crippling failure before having recourse to methods that are good for anybody—strong or weak, advanced or slow?

I demonstrated to you a symbol-picture method as one form of thinking exercise eminently suitable to the age group under consideration. This exercise can be done in the classroom with the chairs in a half circle around the blackboard and the children coming quickly to the board and returning to their seats. Some other thinking games can perhaps be done only in smaller groups. As the children get used to the free atmosphere of thinking, they will be able to work in groups of five to eight with the teacher going from group to group and encouraging their work and helping if the need arises.

In connection with an ongoing *thinking lab* in a school for deaf children, a teacher has for the past year employed a variety of thinking games, some of which I will describe or mention. These games are suitable for all children in the early grades but were specially devised for children who are not particularly adept in linguistic skills. Such children nevertheless spontaneously develop the concepts required by the games and, like other children, are delighted to show off their thinking skills and enjoy being challenged. You will notice that most of the thinking games relate directly to the examples of thinking activities that Piaget observed as typical of the concrete operational child.

1. The *probability* game enjoys popularity from the youngest grade-school age to age eleven. Ten red marbles and ten yellow marbles are spread on a table. The teacher puts eight red marbles and one yellow marble into a bag and shakes it well. The bag is handed from one child to the other; each has to guess the color of the marble he will draw from the bag. After a marble is taken out and its color noted, it is put back into the bag. The little children were greatly surprised that the answer "red" remained the safer bet, draw after draw. The tendency to switch the prediction is very strong. On another trial the children saw that eight red and no yellow balls were put into the bag. Yet some six-year-old children, when they had their turn to pick a marble, still persisted in changing their guess to yellow!

A more advanced modification of the game is to let the bag gradually become empty by putting the chosen marbles on the table. In this way the probability of drawing a red marble will change as the game progresses. With older children it is possible to increase the difficulty of the task by not displaying on the table the marbles that have been taken out. The children have to keep track mentally of the remaining proportion of red and yellow marbles. As a variation, the teacher may use marbles of three different colors or ask for the most reasonable guess if one takes out two marbles at a time.

An ingenious way to help children discover the relation of probability and proportion is to let two or three children observe and keep track of what happens with any proportion of marbles they choose, say 5:2. In addition to the box and the marbles they use a piece of paper divided by a vertical line in the middle. On top they draw five blue circles to the left of the line and two yellow circles to the right. Each child in turn picks a marble and draws a horizontal line, one above the other, to the left or right of the middle line according to the color of the marble. He then puts the marble back into the box, and the next child draws one. As a group of children played this game, they soon observed that the 5:2 proportion was constantly maintained and illustrated by the height of the line columns. At times a child would express the wish to play this game by himself, and with the approval of the teacher he went about being in contact with probability events and chance distributions.

Another variation of the same exercise involved a cardboard circle divided into sectors of uneven size. For a start we had two sectors, one blue, the other yellow. Then we introduced more sectors, with two nonadjacent sectors having the same color. We spun the circle around on a "lazy susan," and the child had to predict which color would be opposite a fixed line outside the circle as it came to a standstill.

2. *Recognizing by touch* is an amusing game that can be modified in many different ways. Its purpose is to sharpen the child's intelligent handling of objects he must recognize by touch. In Piaget's terminology both the visual and the touch perceptions have to be assimilated and transformed into comparable schemes through which the identity of objects can be recognized. In other words, as Piaget frequently points out, an identity judgment is never just a simple recording of perceptual sameness; it is always the result of an operational process.

All you need for this game are a box and two identical collections of small objects, with one collection displayed on a table, the other concealed in the box. The point of the game is to have children look at a single object in one collection and find the identical object by touch alone in the other collection. In order to make the task challenging, the chosen objects are similar in configuration but have small differences. Various kinds of spoons in a variety of designs, sizes, and materials were employed when I watched a group of children playing the game. One child would point to a specific spoon from the collection on the table and indicate to another that he should find this particular spoon by touch from the collection in the box.

All kinds of interesting variations can be built into this game, as a means of challenging the child's thinking. I watched the exercise being done with a collection of small cutout circles of varying sizes, with a collection of cutout triangles differing in shape, and finally with identically shaped pieces of sandpaper of various grades. These were difficult tasks, and even ten-year-old children made lots of mistakes. The transfer from visual to tactile perception can also be reversed. I observed children who had to point to an object on the table identical to the one they had touched in the box. This exercise, too, like the previous one, can be played by the group, or even by one child alone, and can be made more or less difficult so as to challenge the child's capacity for critical differential observation.

3. *Spatial transformations* include a variety of thinking games, all of which boil down to knowing the location of certain points in space relative to other points. These games can be played with the whole class watching the board and each child drawing the required response on a piece of paper.

In the session I watched, the teacher used an overhead projector and drew a certain pattern on the transparency—say, a square. Within the upper left corner of the square she put an *X* and in the lower right corner an *O*. After that she indicated that she would turn the transparency over, first to one side (left), then to another (right), then two more turns (up, down). Each time the children had to draw what the square would look like, and each time the teacher checked the anticipations by turning the transparency over or letting a child do it. The teacher told me about some interesting difficulties. Young children could turn an isosceles triangle up or down. But when two dots and a half circle were put into the triangle to make a face, the children were unable to turn the face. Moreover, the teacher quickly discovered that some figures—a parallelogram, a diamond—were not only difficult to draw when turned around but were difficult to draw at all. These difficulties in orientation are dealt with in Piaget's distinction between figurative and operative, insofar as knowing the outline of a figure *figuratively* is not the same as knowing it *operatively*. A typical seven-year-old child cannot copy a diamond through mere figurative contact and does not yet have the operative knowing of what a diamond is. Only through operative knowing can the child reproduce and transform the figure, because operative knowing means precisely this: to know how a thing is constructed.

In another game of spatial thinking a teacher can have the children reverse sequences of letters, numbers, or what not. When I observed a child reverse BALL into ⅃⅃A𐊒 —with the other children and myself laughing because we expected LLAB—I realized that there is no better way of overcoming reversals in reading and writing than having the child *intentionally* make them. There is also the familiar game of folding a paper and making a cut along the fold. Children are then asked to draw how the paper with the cut will appear when the paper is unfolded.

4. *Communication,* Piaget points out, requires operative understanding and symbolic articulation. This communication game is played by two children, with the others observing and evaluating the performance. The two players sit opposite each other at a small table. On it is a "lazy susan" holding a carboard circle. The circle has four to eight pictures along the margin, all facing out. For instance, it may have a series of identical circles each with a different number of dots within the circle, from few to many. An opaque screen hides the circle from player 2 while player 1 sees the pictures on the circle. The teacher points to one circle. Then the circle is turned around and the screen is reversed so that player 2 sees the pictures. Now player 1, who no longer sees the pictures, has to communicate to player 2 the precise picture to which the teacher pointed. I watched a nine-year-old child who said to his partner, "You see those circles with a bunch of dots. Take the one that has the most dots—you see—then look for the next one—and then the next one, that's the right circle." Another child said, in the same case, "Take the in-between circle." The audience later discussed the effectiveness of communication in terms both of giver and of receiver. The children noted inadequacies, misunderstandings, redundancies; they also pointed out particularly apt expressions.

This task can be varied by limiting communication to a certain number of words, perhaps just two or three. You can also require that only gestures be used, and observe all kinds of imaginative solutions that may pose more problems for the receiver than for the giver. In one session the teacher had prepared a wide variety of picture cards and used them according to the capacity of the children. He noted that younger children invariably produced redundant messages in which the significant cues were buried and therefore frequently missed. He let the children discover that a message limited to the essentials is more effective than a redundant message. The teacher impressed this principle on the children when additional players who did not see the pictures were interspersed between player 1 and player 2. Player 2 and the other children who acted as communicators left the room while player 1 was shown one specific picture from among twelve pictures spread over a table. They were photos of the same person in slightly different positions or clothes. Younger children were not able to keep their communication to the essential point. Thus, by the time the message reached player 2 (the children between took turns at giving and receiving the message), the significant parts had got lost. The children in the audience who observed these events were able to discover on their own the importance of keeping the message down to the essential.

5. *Other thinking games.* I do not wish to turn this into a manual for thinking exercises since my purpose here is merely to give you examples of what can be done in the classroom. There is really no limit to the variety of thinking games. But if a particular game is challenging, the children will spontaneously ask for it again; one does not have to change exercises continually. The teacher in one group intimated that it is usually good practice to stay on a game for several days so that a specific thinking skill can be strengthened and slower children have a chance to catch up. I am quite certain you can discover other thinking games. You can also profitably use some commercial games, as they are or with slight modifications.

Let me mention a few other games we found appropriate for elementary age children. In our thinking lab we used two or three hoops for the purpose of *sorting* or *classifying.* These hoops were put on the floor in partly overlapping position. The children started putting blocks of various sizes, shapes, and colors into appropriate hoops, so that after a few choices a sorting principle emerged which the rest of the children had to follow. The overlapping portions of the hoops were of particular interest. If blue things went into one hoop and round things into another, blue and round things had to be placed in the overlapping section of those two hoops.

Another multiple classification task that enjoyed popularity was a *matrix* task. Use a square, say, of three-by-three fields into which nine objects are to be placed so that from left to right the size of the object increases, and from top to bottom the color gets darker. Other tasks the teacher found appropriate were *pattern* recognition, in which the children had to continue with a once-started pattern, e.g., *x x o x o x x* . . . , or 1, 2, 4, 5, 6, 8 . . . We also adopted some *concept discovery* tasks from the experimental literature by making up a deck of 48 cards with various lines. These lines differed in the following characteristics: (1) straight, curved, or irregular; (2) dark or light; (3) continuous or broken; (4) single or double; and (5) vertical or horizontal. The teacher or child would decide on a certain attribute or combination of attributes. All the cards having these attributes were "correct"; the others were rejected. Cards were shown one after another, and the children had to discover the principle for accepting or rejecting a card. I watched a group of ten-year-old children discover the conjunctive principle "straight *and* dark *and* double lines," after which the teacher switched to the disjunctive principle "irregular *or* broken lines." Although these children had some previous practice in strategies of discovery, it was evident that they needed all the wit at their disposal to make the appropriate discovery.

6. *Visual thinking* characterizes some games I observed while visiting a comprehensive elementary school in Pennsylvania. An imaginative teacher there has expanded the use of visual media into a true program of thinking which, as he remarks, frees the children from the "sit-look-listen syndrome." After working for many years in conventional classrooms, he now has available a beautifully equipped "special experience" room. A dome covers a large circular room around the wall of which eight pictures can be projected. A carpet covers the floor, and light and sound effects can be fully controlled. The children in the room sit on the floor and lean against a movable backrest.

You need not wait until your school has such a room. Everything I describe here can be done in an ordinary classroom, even if not as conveniently. I observed the teacher when he showed to a third-grade class colored slides he had taken while flying from Philadelphia to El Paso, Texas. First he explained to the children that he was going to show them some scenes which he saw during the flight and that he needed the eyes and the intelligence of the children to help him appreciate all the things he saw. Pointing toward the left, he projected the first slide on the wall. It showed the rainy sky over Philadelphia. "Within 30 seconds after takeoff," the teacher said, "we saw this"—pointing to the second slide projected to the right of the first slide. The children were astonished at the contrast: grey and rainy in picture 1, a veritable ocean of sunny clouds in picture 2. After half an hour the cloud formation became less dense (picture 3), and shortly afterward you could see patches of land through a break in the clouds (picture 4). The children were encouraged to express their reactions to what they saw, even to give free rein to their imaginations. The discussion touched on cloud formation, the weather, shadows, light effects, and heights. Presently picture 5 was shown in place of picture 1. Could the children recognize what it showed? There was a winding river, farmlands, sunny and shady parts (caused by what?). What other features could be seen? Each new slide caused lively reactions from some children. The teacher challenged their thinking continually: In which slide was the plane higher? How could they tell? Are there signs of the presence of men and men's work on the rocky plateaus of the Southwest? When seen from afar, where is the center of the city? He showed about 30 slides, and at no time during the 45 minutes was there any letup in the lively discussion.

With another class the teacher employed what he called a "concept" film, that is, a film lasting four to six minutes which repeated itself with no beginning or end and which focused on a certain topic. For instance, to these children of suburbia the teacher showed a film from a street corner in the inner city. The film became the background for a meaningful discussion based on careful observations. During the first few runs of the film the children pointed out interesting facets of street life which a casual look would never have revealed. In due course the children made inferences about the scene and the people they observed: what time of day, what day of the week, what season, where the people lived and worked, why children were not in school during the daytime, and so on. After about 20 minutes another film cartridge was projected that showed life on a street in Calcutta. To everybody's surprise more essential similarities than differences were found when the children compared street scenes from two cities many thousand miles apart.

In making excursions outside the school, films or slides of real life are of special value. They can serve as preparation for an actual visit to one of the pictured scenes or as a follow-up exercise after a visit. But, these pictures, though valuable, are still no substitute for real seeing and contact, which must be the basis for social thinking.

Some of the visual games that I have observed focus directly on the intelligent use of the eyes and are similar to those used in perceptual training. Sometimes the children marked their answers on sheets of paper; at other times they simply talked or pointed to the screen.

Interesting problems included looking for hidden figure—for exam-
.ple, a hammer within a network of different lines—or finding an isolated small part of a whole picture. One specialty of the teacher was
the use of "checkered" cows. He created pictures of cows on which
the pattern of checkered patches could be recognized as definite
pictures—for example, a dog or a duck. The children delighted in
discovering these hidden figures.

There were also matching tasks of all kinds that became increasingly difficult as the alternatives became more nearly alike. Further,
the teacher projected slides on the screen that showed familiar sur-
roundings from unusual viewpoints—for example, a kitchen seen
from the ceiling, a familiar animal from the front or back. Or he
projected a picture out of focus and urged the children to make
reasonable guesses as the picture gradually came into focus. A variation of this game was the presentation of successively more complete
line drawings of familiar objects, with the teacher again encouraging
the children to tell what the complete objects would be.

A different kind of visual exercise dealt primarily with quick, intelligent attention. The teacher would flash digits, geometrical figures,
drawings, or real-life pictures for very short durations. The children
had to recognize and name the projections. I observed a game in
which a series of three figures was flashed against the screen very
briefly and the children had to point out which of the figures was the
odd one.

Many thinking games can be played in small groups or alone. It is
highly recommended that the teacher have available a variety of
activities that can occupy a child who for some reason does not feel
like playing with the group. While young children generally are very
eager to be part of the group, at times they want to be left alone.
Indeed, there may be psychologically sound reasons for the desire to
be alone. I have observed individual children who wanted to work
quietly on some symbol-picture problems, on probability and other
thinking games, or who wanted to watch again some sets of slides
or concept films. By asking for the task these children indicated that
they were involved in it and probably benefitted intellectually from
additional exercise. This opportunity of combining individual and
group work is in part the answer to your question how we can deal
with a group of many children who differ individually in capacity and
interest.

One popular activity is picture completion, an activity that challenges creative thinking and is far to be preferred to traditional coloring exercises. The teacher whose visual thinking program I described converted a small desk into a "light table" by removing the top surface and putting a strong white glass in its place. Underneath he installed two fluorescent lights. By means of various transparencies, many interesting drawing tasks could be devised which exercised visual-motor functioning. Depending on the age and level of the child, he could be challenged by following a dot pattern that made a picture, connecting as fast as possible a pattern of scrambled letters *A* to *Z* (the child himself used a stop watch), or completing a drawing on the basis of a few given lines, and so on and on.

I hope to have shown you, by these few examples, that there is no dearth of thinking exercises. A teacher liberated from the straitjacket of a fixed curriculum can easily employ these games in which the developing intellect of the children is challenged and thereby expanded. It would be premature to ask at this point whether a fixed sequence of exercises is to be recommended particularly since we are limiting our immediate concern to the early elementary grades. Perhaps, as schools of thinking are established, we shall learn by experience which activities are particularly apt and beneficial for certain children. Generally, there is little danger that thinking exercises can be untimely for the simple reason that a child will invariably find his own level along the continuum of difficulties; thus the exercises are as appropriate for the six-year-old as for the nine-year-old.

I would, however, warn you to keep a broad perspective concerning the word "intelligence" and not narrow it down to mere logical reasoning. A child jumping on the trampoline according to a determined pattern—knee drop–swivel hips–front drop–stand–half-turn table–knee drop–back drop–stand—is exercising intelligent control, just as a pianist does when he moves his fingers as the notation requires. Applications of intelligent structures to various forms of human behavior are a normal part of the child's development and constitute just so many occasions for intellectual growth—apart from the variety and richness which they bring into the child's life and the individual variations which they naturally foster. Thus I am anxious to turn in subsequent letters to some of the activities that are not strictly logical but that are very much a part of operative intelligence.

Until next time.

Cordially yours,

creative thinking

LETTER 10

I am glad that you are enjoying my letters. You had no difficulty in seeing the connection between the examples given and the more theoretical part of our previous letters even though I did not spell out in detail the rationale for each exercise. However, you are wondering why I did not mention new curriculum developments designed expressly for elementary schools, such as the modern approaches to math and science or inquiry training. Assuredly, some of our picture logic is not different from notions of set theory employed in modern math teaching. Similarly, the method of thinking games described in the last letter closely resembles some of the most effective ways in which scientific notions about the physical world are transmitted in early grade schools.

As you know, I do not intend to give you anything more than a few practical suggestions of suitable school activities. In the last two letters I purposely chose examples that will be relatively unfamiliar to a teacher and that do not fit the usual curriculum. I will continue to do this for two related reasons. First I would like to see less stress during the early grades on specific subject matter and more emphasis on the general development of the inquiring mind. That an activity is intellectually challenging should be enough for it to be welcomed in

116

education; it need not constantly be justified on account of its being part of a certain curriculum to be learned.

But, more important, focusing on a certain curriculum in quantitative terms of cumulative information puts the classroom teacher into a dilemma; the result usually is that figurative content, unfortunately, wins over operative thinking. Thus, from what I have seen, modern math and science have been admirably planned to deemphasize rote memorization and to encourage mathematical and scientific thinking. In some of these endeavors Piaget's ideas have been used to good purpose. Yet, I think, the full benefit of these thinking curricula will only be realized if they form part of an educational structure that consistently favors thinking over content. In the meantime, we realize that many so-called modern math courses stress the rote learning of rules and content, just as the "old" math did.

The activity I am about to describe not only does not fit into the usual subject matter but is not even directly concerned with logical thinking. I observed it on a visit to a third-grade classroom where a drama teacher held a class of 26 girls and boys spellbound for two hours. He asked the children to form groups of four or five. Each group was to discuss among themselves and decide on playing a "real" event in which the members of the group were to act as real people. The word "real" was stressed. I was given to understand that earlier in the year the children had favored playing imaginary events and persons.

The teacher pointed to one group, which quickly disappeared behind a screen. There the children found a variety of costumes, wigs, play telephones, sticks, and so on. They could help themselves. The only other materials specially made for the occasion were six wooden boxes of various sizes. The sides of some of the boxes were open so that one could step into them. The boxes were arranged by the players before the start of the play to become part of a scene. (The teacher afterward told me that even these props are not necessary and that for two years he managed very well without them.)

The rest of the children and the teacher were the audience. Their job was to participate in the play. The teacher would encourage the children to pay attention and keep remarks until the end. "We need your eyes and your advice. So watch and tell us at the end," he would say to the watching children. He would also talk to the players (side coaching) in order to help the acting along ("Keep telling us what you see from the bus"), to encourage ("Act your age!"), or even to suggest modifications of the entire scene.

The first group of four children called "curtain." One boy sat down on a small box which was placed on a bigger box. This boy was obviously driving a motor vehicle. Soon it became clear that he was driving a bus. He used the gears, clutch, and brakes and hummed continuously to imitate the motor.

The bus came to a stop and three girls entered. The third one paid for the tickets and announced, "The art museum, please." The three people, who seemed to be a mother with two young girls, sat down on boxes behind the driver. The bus started off, and in a few seconds the driver announced, "Art museum." At this point the teacher interjected: "Freeze! How long does it take to get from the original place to the museum? Take your time. If it takes only a few seconds, who would take the bus? Start again and keep in mind a real ride."

The children went behind the screen for a minute and started afresh. They improved the precision of acting by having a conversation at the bus stop before entering the bus. It became clear that a mother, a daughter, and her girl friend were going to the museum. They rode along with the bus driver, who bounced in his seat to show that the ride was bumpy. An impatient child in the audience reminded the passengers that if the driver's seat bounces, the passengers' seats usually bounce all the more.

This time the drive lasted considerably longer. The girls talked to each other about the museum. The mother, noting that it was hot in the bus, opened the window. When the bus stopped and the driver announced, "Museum," the passengers asked, "Which one?" The driver replied, "This is the technical museum." So the passengers continued to the next stop and then got off the bus, leaving by a side door.

The bus drove on. The teacher suggested a one-minute intermission to allow the players to rearrange the scene for the museum. He also urged the bus driver of the first scene to join the three persons in visiting the gallery.

The next scene showed the art museum. As the three visitors wandered from one picture to the next, the bus driver took on the role of guide. He pointed out the particular qualities of each picture. The visitors admired the pictures and exhibited a variety of reactions. Finally the guide took them to a very precious picture protected from the light by a curtain. (The teacher reminded them to work out an ending within a minute.) The guide moved the curtain and noticed to his horror that the picture had been stolen. He ran off immediately to let the police know. The mother and her daughter followed the guide shortly. The friend stayed behind. Looking with curiosity around the place where the missing picture belonged, she discovered it lying on the ground. As she ran off with the precious picture in her hand, the teacher called "curtain" and the play was ended.

The teacher turned to all the children, audience and players. What did they like in the play and why? Was there any acting that was out of character? Did the actors show us who they were? Did they make the scene seem real?

One child remarked that he liked the bus ride but it was not real because the players alone were in the bus. But other children interjected, "This is possible. I was once in a bus alone with Mom and Dad." Another child expressed surprise that it should be hot in the bus because the actors were wearing furs and hats. Apparently it was winter time. But then again they kept these things on in the museum, and was that not rather unusual? The group agreed that it was unusual but not implausible. A third child brought up another point. The changes of gears were not sufficiently realistic; buses had four gears, and the driver had used only two.

The teacher asked about the museum scene. Well, stealing the picture and finding it was fun. Could this really have happened? Some children objected to the good behavior of the two girls in the play. "They did not behave like real children." "Did anybody notice how the guide ran away from the scene?" asked the teacher. "Yes, he ran right through there." "But was there not supposed to be a wall?" The children laughed. "He must have run through the wall. He did not make the wall real."

This scene lasted about 15 minutes, and then another group was invited to come onstage. They acted a scene that was afterward evaluated as rather improbable: Children going for a walk and suddenly discovering a space ship on the playground. Another group of boys acted the robbery of a jewel that was kept in a warehouse. In this scene one of the more difficult parts was "playing dead." The teacher said to the boy lying on the floor, "You help the scene by lying still." But it was not easy for an energetic boy to lie there and let other boys buffet him. Eventually he did get up, and he tried to compensate for the impropriety of coming back to life by playing a ghost. A fourth group acted a scene with Snoopy the dog in a rocket. When it was over, the children realized that they had not solved the problem posed; these were not real people but characters of the comic strip.

Before I tell you more about the drama technique, as I learned it from conversation with the teacher, I would like to show you in what manner operative intelligence became manifest in the children's acting. You remember how Piaget discussed the functioning of symbolic play in the young child. In play the child assimilates an external event to a scheme of knowing that is of momentary interest. A particular interest may fortuitously be triggered by the presence of some external thing. For instance, a child, seeing and grasping a block on a table, starts playing car with it. Piaget suggests therefore that in early symbolic play assimilation dominates accommodation. That is, the child in spontaneous play does not accommodate to a set task, but uses the situation symbolically in the service of his knowing of cars.

There is a difference between spontaneous play and play-acting. In the first case the child assimilates a situation without making a corresponding accommodation; he plays, we say, as his fancy strikes him. In the acting I observed, there was a problem to be solved. The acting becomes the means by which the child accommodates to the problem. Let us take a child acting "How old am I?" He sits on a bench at a bus stop waiting for the bus. The children in the audience have to discover the age from observing the actor. The teacher softly coaches the child: "Feel your age." "Let your knees feel your age." "Let your hands feel your age." Only the teacher and the acting child know how old he is to be. The teacher does not tell the child *what* he feels or *how* to act the age. He merely reminds him to let his bodily behavior express what *he* personally knows about that age. This knowing is not something that the young child, or perhaps anybody else, has available as a neatly packaged piece of information. It is a knowing based on experience of self and others that perhaps only a gifted writer is able to put into words. It is, moreover, a knowing that literally becomes and never simply exists statically, precisely because it deals with unique personal experiences.

It is hard for an adult to verbalize, in discursive fashion, the knowing under discussion. Thus it is doubly appropriate to give young children an opportunity to symbolize knowing by acting. Let us watch the child, a third-grade boy. He sits rather rigidly stiff. At the teacher's coaching ("Let your knees feel the age"), he puts one leg across the other. He keeps looking at his watch and every now and then stretches his neck in the direction from which he expects the bus to come.

One can observe how the child's knowing about the age of 40 is being shaped in the process of acting.

A child in the audience lifts his hand. "I think he acts the age of a teenager." "What did he show to make you think that?" asks the teacher. "He looked at his watch because he has a date." "Is there no other reason for looking at the watch?" The children think about that. The teacher suggests to the actor, "Continue and show your age in your face." The child acting a 40-year-old man puts on a stern face. A child in the audience cries out, "He is a grown-up." Another child shouts, "He is fifty years old." Then teacher, the player, and the audience together evaluate the performance. They compare the acting to that in the two previous problems, where the ages portrayed were four years and 80 years.

In every way, both as actors and as audience, the children are applying their operative knowing to the symbolic acting. The teacher accepts no cheap stereotype or half-baked solution. For instance, when the child thought a teenager was waiting at the bus stop, the teacher asked for evidence. Observation is here linked with intelligence: the children can use their own experience for the intelligent solving of a given problem.

Once the children get accustomed to this task, it gives them opportunities for creative thinking rarely provided by the spontaneous environment. We tend to think of creativity as an exception limited to specially talented children. Acting can give ordinary children a taste of controlling their bodily movements and actions according to their intuitive knowing of situations. The initial vagueness of knowing becomes articulated in a constructive, task-oriented group atmosphere. The actors who are being evaluated are not simply performers to be judged. They, together with the audience and the teacher, are participating in the evaluation and have the satisfaction of a task well done. Moreover—and this is very important—there is never just one correct solution. It is, therefore, not a question of just doing *the* right thing. Even more important is that, strictly speaking, there are no wrong solutions. As long as the acting shows what it is meant to show, as long as the symbols transmit the agreed-on message, the acting is right and the solution is correct.

The main difference between symbolic play of early childhood and improvised acting is the controlled application of knowing-schemes to the set task in all parts of the body, in each movement and behavioral sequence. The children themselves are quick to appreciate the difference between whimsical play and purposeful acting. Just as in the thinking games the children did not merely *play* thinking but were seriously *engaged* in thinking, here too they were not merely *pretending* but *giving reality to objects.* Knowing and reality are correlative terms: an object is not real to us unless it is in some way actively known by us. Knowing is thus an engaging business, and when there is engagement, there is motivation, interest, "real fun."

In one scene children acted tug-of-war. The teacher remarked to me, "If a child is not physically exhausted at the end of the scene, just as he would be in real life, you know that he was not doing the task well." When a child on the stage looked around instead of actively participating, the teacher needed only to remind him in words like this: "There are actors on the stage and there is the audience in the room. If you would rather watch than act, you may do so by joining the audience." This sufficed to turn the child to the task without scolding him or making him feel in the wrong.

I was particularly impressed how the teacher handled more serious problems of discipline. During a scene one of the five boys on the stage lost a shoe. The other boys in the scene started giggling and making silly remarks. The teacher reached for a play telephone that was handy and spoke to the players on stage as if he were part of the game: "Jim, can you hear me?" The actors looked toward the teacher. "I just saw a funny boy walking down the street with only one shoe on. Ha, ha, he really does look silly. Watch out for him." Jim, one of the actors, immediately took up the challenge and incorporated the teacher's remarks into the scene. The result? Instead of a lecture of disapproval, the giggling became part of the play. In this connection the teacher warned me that in some classes, particularly during the early stages, one should expect rough situations that must be handled with tact and good grace. Many children are unaccustomed to the experience of freedom within a task-oriented setting. For them, to be free means to hit, push, kick, and run. To be in school means to be silent and passively listening. A game situation where initiative is asked for and rewarded is a new experience for them. It takes time for the children and the teacher to learn how to handle this type of situation.

I discussed with the teacher the philosophy underlying the drama technique. He showed me a book by Viola Spolin *(Improvisation for the Theater,* Evanston, Ill., Northwestern University Press, 1963; excerpts reprinted with permission) that provides a detailed account of the techniques as applied to adults and children. As I browsed through the book I found more psychological soundness than in many a psychology course taught at the college level. Listen to some excerpts on creativity and discipline and notice how they corroborate what we said about operative knowing in contrast to the dangers of a static, low-operative knowing, which is frequently due to a misplaced use of the linguistic medium.

"If the teacher-director forces set patterns of thinking and behavior (a 'right' or 'wrong' way of doing things) on his child actors, he is restricting them most severely. . . . Children, who are our future, are talked at so much that a great many adult formulations are either lost to them entirely or swallowed whole, undigested and unquestioned." The author, recalling that many newcomers to the theater are heard to say, "You mustn't turn your back to the audience," continues, "Here, on the very threshold of learning, a door is shut and obviously by one who doesn't have the faintest idea of what he is saying and is simply passing on something he has heard or thinks is so. In how many other areas must this go on, hour after hour, day after day, in a child's life?" (pp. 285–86).

All I can add is that schools must not compound this general cultural situation of imposing ready-made formulas and "summaries of another's findings" on the growing intellect by an early education that stresses linguistic skills unduly. A good part of language consists in ready-made formulas. You can see that the author of the book, without being directly interested in scholastic success, came independently to the same conclusion about language and creative acting that we reached regarding language and intellectual development. This is, of course, more than a coincidence because creativity and intelligence are really the same thing. It is only our lopsided preoccupation with certain static facets of intelligence that has made it possible and indeed necessary to focus on creativity *apart* from intelligence. When the author points out that "creativity is not rearranging; it is transformation" (p. 42), she is speaking exactly as Piaget would speak about operative intelligence. You recall that in his theory of knowing an operative act is the active assimilation and transformation of given data according to the structural forms available to the child. In many places Piaget criticizes the view that considers intelligence to be merely a clever rearranging or organizing of basic bits of information.

The drama technique not only brings out operative creativity within the child, but also carries with it a basic motivation that is intrinsic to the activity, as in the development of the intelligence. Any healthy child enjoys acting, for acting means showing his knowing for the joy of sharing it with others. Discipline problems that arise during schooling are frequently symptoms of a malfunctioning behavioral situation which chokes intrinsic motivation. Spolin rightly equates discipline and active involvement. Here again you can see how close her opinion is to the view that contrasts low-operative, figurative knowing to involved, high-operative knowing. Contrary to theories of learning that place motivation outside the learning process, involved operative knowing is its own reward and is the precondition for any true creative discipline. When this situation is lacking, any so-called discipline may be merely a superficial coping technique. Take the case of the proverbial good boy who "may simply be intent upon getting reward instead of punishment, approval instead of disapproval. He seeks survival by appeasement. The so-called undisciplined child is seeking survival also; he, however, is in rebellion against . . . restrictions he does not understand . . . " (p. 287).

The thinking expressed in these sentences is not new. Yet teachers have never really been able to benefit from its implication as long as they have had to act within the traditional system. For far too many youngsters our educational system, with its primary reliance on extrinsic motivation, has stifled intrinsic motivation. A discipline that is emotionally healthy is a discipline based on involvement. A rational procedure for education would be to focus on involvement, that is, on an activity which *by itself* implies involvement, such as operative thinking in its various forms. As we saw earlier, the notion that creativity is something apart from intelligence impoverishes the fullness of both intelligence and creativity. Similarly, the idea that motivation is something to be added to the functioning intelligence implies a static view of intelligence which neglects the intrinsic source of intellectual development.

One further aspect is well illustrated by dramatic improvisation, and it is as much a part of operative intelligence as are creativity and intrinsic motivation. I refer here to the group aspect of the game situation. All acting is a group activity. The scenes I described at the beginning of this letter resulted from a group consensus. In fact, even the single acting of the game "How old am I?" is subject to rules and evaluations that are accepted by all. Audience, players, and teacher participate in the group and contribute their indispensable part to the functioning of the group. "Any game worth playing is highly social and has a problem that needs solving within it—an objective point in which each individual must become involved . . . " (p. 5). In my next letter I want to say more about this objectivity so as to forestall erroneous notions about it. Many people consider social cooperation and individual operative thinking to be somehow opposites instead of two sides of the same coin. There cannot be individual thinking without social thinking, nor can one say that one causes or comes before the other. For the time being I want you to accept that acting fosters an objective viewpoint which derives from group acceptance and concentration on the task. Without being bound by logical objectivity, creative dramatic acting is diametrically opposed to an individualistic subjectivism free of rules.

In a setting of dramatic creativity the restricting tendency to compete for success and to compare one's performance with that of others can give way to a healthy collaboration. The process of solving the problem together comes before the end-result, the solution. "If we are trained only for success, then to gain it we must necessarily use everyone and everything for this end; we may cheat, lie, crawl, betray, or give up all social life to achieve success. How much more certain would knowledge be if it came from and out of the excitement of learning itself. How many human values will be lost and how much will our art forms be deprived if we seek only success?" (p. 12).

You must have noticed that the atmosphere underlying group acting is most conducive to healthy social development and could be advocated for this reason alone. Indeed, drama technique is used in some schools as a means of training children in sensitivity to others and increased self-expression. These benefits are so obvious that I would like to put a greater emphasis on the close relation between creative acting and operative intelligence. People who are used to evaluating things in terms of the end-product ask me what is the purpose of training in symbol logic if it is not knowledge of symbol logic. I reply to this that I am interested not in teaching logic directly but in the process of thinking that is operative when the child grapples with given problems. Similarly, people are inclined to say that drama is good because it teaches poise and self-expression. But I want you to understand clearly that I am suggesting drama techniques to you primarily as thinking activities that *in themselves* are challenging and conducive to a healthy development.

The teacher whose activity I observed also mentioned to me that drama techniques have been successfully employed to achieve certain required curriculum results. I repeat this to you with some hesitation, not because there is anything wrong in using the game "What am I doing?" in connection with teaching spelling but for reasons mentioned at the beginning of the letter. This game is an excellent thinking exercise by itself and does not need the justification of perhaps providing motivation for learning to spell. Whereas there is no danger in the fact that a good individual teacher will play the game well and at the same time get some spelling across, I am skeptical of a system that accepts drama techniques or any of the illustrative thinking activities primarily in order to help the traditional curriculum. In due course, thinking becomes a luxury that is dispensable and the desired result remains a drill to be imposed regardless of the psychological condition of the individual children.

You ask me how this spelling game is played. One child is chosen and decides on a certain activity—washing dishes, mowing the lawn, teaching school. He tells the teacher his choice. The teacher coaches the child in acting this activity so that it can be distinguished from other activities that look superficially like it. As soon as a child in the audience thinks he knows the name of the activity, he writes the appropriate words on the board. If his guess is correct, he joins the first child in a related activity. For instance, if the original player washes dishes, other children might act drying dishes, cleaning the stove, defrosting the refrigerator, and so on.

A more highly developed version of the game would require that players new to the scene interact with those already on stage. For example, the first player is a teacher, the second is a child taking instructions from the teacher, the third is a parent inquiring about a child, the fourth is a supervising teacher, and so forth.

You can see that this game lends itself to helping children realize characteristic features of certain activities and things. Spelling these things on the blackboard need not necessarily spoil the sense of the game. But all along the teacher must remember that this is not a spelling lesson and that a misspelled word must be corrected without squelching the excitement of the group.

This is, of course, the secret of all good teaching. If the intrinsic motivation of thinking (= excitement) can be kept alive in a particular learning process, success is practically ensured. In this sense the drama technique, as practiced by an experienced teacher, appears to me an outstanding example of a good learning situation. If you should be interested in reading the book by Spolin, keep in mind that it was not concerned with traditional educational goals. Nevertheless, it is a veritable mine of fruitful psychological applications if it can be viewed within the framework of the development of operative intelligence. If you can share this viewpoint with me, you will have gone once and for all beyond the confines of a narrowly conceived logical intelligence, understanding that intelligence is not a cold, static function by which we reason in abstract isolation. The insight that intelligence implies involvement, development, and creativity is perhaps the most important discovery you can make from our continuing correspondence.

All best wishes.

Yours sincerely,

social thinking

LETTER 11

Dear Teacher:

Not surprisingly, you saw many more variations and functions to which the drama technique can be put. I wish you could have talked yourself to the teacher whose enthusiasm for the technique seemed boundless. He thought he could teach any curriculum or subject matter through drama. You point out to me that this technique would lend itself beautifully to making children actively aware of social and moral questions long before they could verbalize them in discursive fashion. You also mention that when you visited some elementary schools in the inner-city area, you thought how the ideas laid out in our correspondence could be put into practice.

You are right that it is in these schools that education's most important impact will have to be made. Yet, even while I am writing, it becomes clear to me that the one field in which education has been least successful applies as well to schools of the middle class. This general failure presents perhaps a bigger challenge to education than the failure in inner-city schools. The obvious change that can be suggested for the city schools would imply a change in matters of the mind—more emphasis on thinking and less on specific skills. But *all* schools, in fact, have failed to awaken in the great majority of people the urgent concerns of

128

justice, compassion, and human dignity that must be present in abundance if our democratic system is to prosper and function for the benefit of present and future generations. Our society needs a change of heart—and this is harder to come by than a change of curriculum.

People may balk when a change of educational system is suggested, but they may eventually feel consoled at the prospect of seeing the kind of individuals whom traditional educational methods wanted but failed to produce. Now, I suggest to you a much more radical innovation, the training of individuals who are constantly encouraged to think and to apply this thinking not merely to science, letters, or the creative arts, but quite consciously to social and moral life, to the relation of man to his fellow men and his society and to relations among societies.

You said that a teacher in Harlem referred to Piaget's theory of knowing as *liberating* because, in Piaget's perspective, learning is not an event imposed from the outside to be manipulated according to an arbitrary standard of an individual or a group. In fact, creative learning involves what is deepest and most objective in the human being. Operative knowing in Piaget's sense is involved knowing. It is through assimilation by action-schemes of knowing that the individual is put into contact with the environment. Until now we have apparently focused on knowing in relation only to the physical environment. We have learned that for Piaget knowing becomes stable and objective to a degree commensurate with the active contribution of the subject (the person who knows). Freedom of critical thinking involves the active participation of the thinking subject. With regard to physical reality, such freedom implies a subjection to and reverence for critical truth.

What does operative freedom imply vis-à-vis social reality? This question is much more difficult to answer, simply because social reality embraces human persons in their concrete relation to other persons. Our knowing of and dealing with persons can never reach the level of abstract logical certainty that we can apply to physical reality. Nonetheless, our intellect is not meant to stop working when it comes to social relations. On the contrary, history tells us that the farthest-reaching effects of intellectual achievements eventually became manifest in a change of society's (that is, the typical individual's) view of the human person. This view is a complex network of values, interests, customs, and habits handed on to society's younger generations in a heritage of implicit, unanalyzed knowing. There can be no doubt in anybody's mind that, over the years since World War II, enormous changes in society have taken place. These changes are not limited to our country. Repercussions of a changing social outlook are felt in every part of the globe. Thinking people recognize the inadequacies of present social structures—but where can we look for definite answers? I do not know, but one thing is sure: No constructive answer to the exigencies of social life will be forthcoming if ordinary citizens do not apply their intellect to social reality with the same fervor and the same commitment as some researchers in the past have done to physical reality. Society could produce great scientists and great artists even if only a small proportion of its people received a formal education. Today, however, the greatest need is not for individual scientists to make startling discoveries but for the masses of people—the product of mass education—to live and enjoy life together as fully valued human beings. This state of affairs will not come about unless each person consciously and responsibly applies his intellect to the real problems of society. At the same time, an intellectual development that stops short of the social reality is bound to be experienced today as incomplete and irrelevant.

Education for thinking, therefore, has as its most important indirect goal helping individuals to take an active, intelligent part in shaping the life of society, from personal relations within a family to attitudes toward people living in other countries and under different social systems. As with other activities, the age range of the elementary school period is a most necessary and at the same time a most promising period for laying the foundation of social thinking.

The thinking of a teenager or a young college student should not have to be rudely awakened by something like the intellectual shock that occurs when his uncritcally accepted social structures are suddenly viewed as fallible, partial solutions. These young people justifiably resent having been kept in the dark so long, and educational institutions will be one target of their resentment. Other youngsters repress the shock and, using a defense mechanism to protect their personal integrity, reject tenaciously any idea of social change. And a third large group of men and women remain throughout life passive recipients of the social pressures around them. Resentment, repression, and a "low-level operative" noninvolvement are hardly attitudes that are socially healthy and constructive.

The period before school age is not an optimal time to intervene in social education because structures for stable thinking have not yet been developed. This intervention is not meant to take place in a formal, didactic manner. Rather, the child should be exposed to the social and moral environment of his culture and given opportunities to apply his intellectual operations in this area. Some of Piaget's keenest observations relate to the young preschool child's construction of reality as a strange twilight where "all is necessary and all is possible." Things are there, events happen, and the child thinks that everything takes place because it must be so. At the same time the little child's picture of the world is so fluid that practically anything could happen without occasioning much surprise. But at age six or seven the child constructs his first stable notions. He is beginning to comprehend intellectually the bewildering variety of the constantly changing physical environment. These notions Piaget calls "operations." They permit the individual to make mental experiments and eventually to regard physical reality not so much as something given but rather as concrete instances from among many theoretical possibilities.

Social reality is, of course, part of the environment in which every child grows up. The child accepts it as unquestioningly as he accepts physical events. Moreover, his primary personal relations, which help him grow intellectually, are with his peers. In social interaction with his peers he grows up and reaches the intellectual stage of operations. In this sense Piaget's theory is as applicable to social as to physical reality. The child becomes part of the community of thinking individuals as he applies his operational structures to a variety of physical problems, depending on given situations. Similarly, he becomes an active part of the community of social individuals as he applies these structures to social problems. In the first case we speak of "operations"; in the case of society we call it "cooperation." Piaget delights in the semantic coincidence (or is it more than coincidence?) that structures of reversible operations applied to society become structures of reciprocal cooperation.

The first requirement of an elementary school for thinking is to expose the growing intelligence to existing social structures. Children can be encouraged to explore their immediate environment in a manner that will not merely give them a figurative knowing of things here and now, but will provide opportunities for operative development. By figurative knowing, as you are already aware, I refer to a low-level operative knowing focused on external, figurative constellations, such as knowing that a store is open from 9 a.m. to 9 p.m. or that a bank has a safety vault. Far too many so-called field trips turn out to be mere collecting of figurative knowing and as a consequence do not engage or even much interest the individual child. An overall result of neglect inside and outside the school is widespread indifference toward the social structures. They are simply accepted and are of no particular concern to the intelligence of the growing child.

Do you realize what I am implying? We hear the words "alienated" and "irrelevant" applied to our educational establishment from the graduate right down to elementary schools. Unless I am mistaken, the primary cause for this malaise is dissatisfaction with existing social structures. The alienated intellect considers these structures irrelevant in the precise sense that they do not provide food for intellectual assimilation now, and never have. They appear incomprehensible and strange, something imposed from outside and not an organic part of one's self. You remember that all along Piaget stresses that knowing means actively working or mentally operating on something. It is my thesis that a great number of our young people are alienated because they are intellectually starved. There are so many things in the modern physical or social environment that children cannot spontaneously assimilate. Our schools have a clear and urgent task to help our children feel intellectually at home in the world they live in.

If we can link operative thinking with contact in the social environment, we accomplish three vital things for the healthy development of the child. First, we help him grow intellectually by giving him occasions to which his knowing structures can be applied. Second, we introduce the child into social realities as an active participant. We give him to understand that, like physical reality, social realities are not simply given, but result from and require the intelligent contribution of individual persons. Finally, we can reasonably expect that as these children grow up, they will be prepared to work for the urgent concerns of society that will continue to emerge under the rapidly changing conditions of modern life.

When I speak in this vein to socially concerned leaders, I am constantly asked, "But can we afford to wait until today's children have grown up to become tomorrow's leaders?" This question is really beside the point. I am not saying that my ideas on early education are an adequate answer to all our present social problems. But surely education of our young children must become responsive to these problems, and the sooner the better. If grade-school education in the fifties had been more relevant for the active operations and cooperations required by our changing times, who knows that the sixties might not have been more constructive and promising? Since we do have young children in school today, we should make every conceivable effort to provide an education that will help them exercise their developing operative intelligence on the burning questions of today's social and political life, in order to prepare them for the questions of tomorrow. On this point there can be no doubt. The chances of successfully building up a worthy and constructive human life at the age period of six to ten years is immeasurably higher and incomparably less expensive than similar "salvaging" efforts at a later period.

I am afraid I have said many speculative things, and it is time to come down to practical reality. What should we as teachers do? I wish I could give you many precise examples rather than a general perspective. However, I can think of three broad areas of the social and moral life that should be articulated for the thinking child. Let us call these areas the obvious, the disguised, and the hidden social environment.

Excursions out of the classroom should be an ordinary part of the school day, not something special that happens a few times during the year. The purpose should be to familiarize the school child with his immediate social and physical environment. We teachers will soon find that we do not have all the answers and that our social awareness is woefully inadequate. For instance, it is well documented that we do not know basic facts about how people within our own community live when they belong to a social class other than our own. White, middle-class individuals do not understand life in the city ghetto, and ghetto inhabitants have a distorted image of the middle class. Or, on a much more mundane level, do we know how food is distributed to the food store, how it is kept and disposed of if not sold?

As in other thinking exercises, you may not be able to take a whole class to a certain place, but you can try to have all children share in the experience. I observed a teacher who, together with her second-grade children, made up a list of places, events, or people which the children encounter in their daily lives. This list included such things as a grocery store, the mailman, the bank, a policeman, the bus driver, the garage, the drug store, a doctor, a real estate office. The important thing was to engage the children's interest and to avoid giving them ready-made answers.

The teacher told me that generally visits can easily be arranged. Working people take a certain pride in explaining to youngsters what job they are doing and why. During the visit the teacher stayed in the background and let the children do the talking. Her main job was to be attentive to the children's interest and to encourage the questioning. She brought a camera along so that the children could take pictures.

When the visit was over, there followed the most important part of the trip, discussion and evaluation. The teacher became a discussion leader and a secretary (and, by writing down and reading things children reported, the teacher provided encouragement toward learning to read). The questions at first are bound to be on a very simple level. The teacher recorded them, together with the answers, and helped the children to evaluate them. Were the questions relevant? Did the answers make the event real? (Remember that "to make real" is to "make known.") She then helped the children to pull together the answers. The teacher must be satisfied with a bare minimum of well articulated knowing and must convince herself and the children that the questioning itself is more important than the memorizing of the answer. One question spontaneously asked and answered is of more value than any number of answers to questions that are imposed on the child. Instead of asking ourselves, what does a child know? (which may merely elicit a low-level operative answer), we should focus on the operative use of his intelligence: Does the child ask questions that manifest his intellectual level?

I also heard children ask questions about things in their own home. When the teacher did not know the answer, she said so unashamedly. When she did know, she was slow in giving a purely verbal answer. I was present when a child asked her about the functioning of a refrigerator, and I was relieved when she declined to explain with verbal discourse and diagrams.

In another classroom I observed a teacher who turned the customary "show-and-tell" into occasions for meaningful social thinking. The children had decided to bring along some piece of mail from home. The teacher helped the children to classify these pieces, and the children were grouped accordingly. In one corner we had children with personal letters, in another children with bills or business letters; a third group had advertisements, and a fourth group had magazines and parcels. Each group was to pick two pieces that seemed especially interesting. The teacher moved from group to group and helped the children to reach decisions and to justify their choices. Each group in turn presented its two pieces of mail and with the discreet help of the teacher replied to the questions of the other children. There was an old birthday card from a relative in Canada, a paid bill for electricity, an advertisement of a newly established hardware store, and a national magazine. By means of these items many spontaneous views about the social environment became articulated and could be amplified or, if need be, corrected. But the controlling factor in this discussion was the peer group rather than the authority of the teacher.

In connection with knowing your home and your neighborhood, the drama technique which we discussed in the previous letter is particularly useful. One teacher told me how the children acted "house," each group of children representing things in a particular room. Was any important thing left out? Not infrequently, children acted something for which they did not know the right name. One teacher I spoke to used to take children on excursions to a real-life scene (a park, a bus stop) for the express purpose of having them observe the situation. They would then decide on a certain theme to be improvised later in dramatic play. This play led quite naturally to the evaluating and questioning of social structures and contributed to the children's feeling at home in their environment.

By means of these and other techniques the "obvious" environment can be linked with the general thinking atmosphere of the school. I grant you that these topics are frequently mentioned in our elementary schools although usually in a manner that is much too descriptive and verbal. We have employed the term "low-level operative" for such activities. On the other hand, the main forces underlying life in the neighborhood are seldom discussed. I refer here to the "disguised" environment (from which we tend to protect and insulate our children), including social situations and events that shape the community in which the children live. It seems to me that, particularly on this score, a teacher cannot close the door to discussion as long as the topic is part of the child's spontaneous inquiry. The words the child hears at home, vaguely comprehends, and more frequently distorts should not be excluded from the early school years. On the contrary, the child is now ready and open to accept and face reality as he will never accept it again. We teachers can guide children toward the reality underlying such words as race and discrimination, poverty and welfare, jobs and unemployment, physical and mental illness, crime and drinking, war and peace.

When the school is regarded primarily as a place that presents the child with certain fixed knowledges that he is to retain, it is no wonder that we are anxious to omit any mention of these and similar words. As with religious or sex education, we respect the right of the individual and the family, and we may instinctively abhor any tendency to impose certain value systems on the young child. However, we here consider the school as a situation in which the thinking of the child is encouraged to operate and to develop. For us a teacher's job is not to give value judgments but to help children realize the moral responsibility behind everyday, common events. As in our logical thinking exercises, we do not suggest the imposition of ready-made answers. According to their capacity, children can be guided to discover and apply the invariants of "objective" reasoning—logical rules and symbolic articulation—and in the social area they can be led to recognize the invariant factors underlying social responsibility. These factors can be summed up as the moral dignity of the human person.

Characteristically, Piaget in his probing of the child's mind has not neglected the moral field. In fact, through his writings he has contributed greatly to a more balanced understanding of children's sense of morality. Some experimental educational programs make use of Piaget's suggested stages of moral development, or a modified version of them, but they focus on an age level higher than grade school. Piaget has shown that one cannot expect a mature, verbalized judgment before the formal operational stage—that is, the period when one's thinking structures are appropriately expressed in verbal propositions and bear directly on hypothetical situations. He has stressed that here, particularly, verbal formulations lag behind concrete behavior and that premature verbalizations run the risk of contributing toward an adult morality that remains immature.

Consequently, in matters of moral judgment the ideal teacher (he may not exist, but the educational structure should encourage and not suppress approaches to the ideal) will continue to conduct himself in the same way he did in the previous thinking or drama exercises. He is not there primarily to give information, although he strives for a respectable measure of objectivity when social facts and statistics are important. It is a safe rule to avoid all explicit comparative judgments that call one thing good and another bad, because such articulation of value judgments (like definitions) belongs at the end of a person's development, not at the beginning. We strive here to open the discussion, particularly among peers, so that the child begins to question and work on value judgments that will eventually be *his*.

The last area that I relate to social thinking is what I called the "hidden" environment. It encompasses factors that determine, individually and socially, our style of life. They are responsible for our deepest convictions, our unanalyzed assumptions, our preferred values. These forces influence the social environment of the school and the classrooms. It is proper for a teacher to ask himself what message he conveys to the children. Is it a message that shows he accepts the personality of the child, that encourages the child's social and intellectual development?

We know that educators in a long tradition have put primary stress on such factors as personal acceptance, and I would be the last to belittle them. However, I venture to suggest that sensitivity to the "hidden" environment is not enough for a successful school. "Love is not enough" for the hungry child; he needs wholesome food on the table. Educational theories have been on a perilous swing from an extreme that stressed discipline and learning to another that focused on emotional and social adjustment. I suggest that you cannot have one without the other. A viable theory of the development of knowing will also be a viable theory of emotional and social development. A school system whose goal is geared toward healthy intellectual growth cannot but be conducive to healthy emotional and social growth. For this reason alone, my professional advice on problems of educational adjustment or motivation would be first to check the objective program that is offered to the child. If this program is psychologically or socially unsuitable to a child's developing intelligence, we should be slow in looking for secondary, indirect causes.

These few observations merely sketch ideas on the vast topic of social thinking. All I want to show you is the close organic connection between intelligence and social reality. If the school is to be for real, intellectual food must be for real, too. This implies, particularly at the age level of early operational intelligence (ages six to nine), active intellectual exploration and evaluation of the social environment. I hope that with your help, and with the help of others who are concerned about the child and his relation to society, the day is not far off when these ideas can be elaborated and put into practice. For this purpose even more than for other reasons, we need primary school programs that subordinate all activities to the criterion of healthy operative development.

Many educators have social concerns not unlike those expressed in this letter. The one new thing I hope to bring to their attention is Piaget's overarching approach to the development of the child. If, in our previous discussions, the word "intellectual" appeared to be overstressed in contrast to "social" or "emotional," this was simply because the rules of logical intelligence can be clearly articulated. But bear in mind that underlying all forms of human behavior are structures of intelligent knowing. Many specific skills that are considered a "must" in traditional education are dispensable as far as healthy development is concerned. However, operative thinking with regard to the physical, social, and personal-moral reality is an indispensable characteristic of human growth. In this sense Piaget's theory is not merely a theory of intellectual development; it is quite properly a theory of *human* development and as such unifies the various activities we have called logical, creative, and social.

My very best wishes.

Sincerely yours,

musical thinking

LETTER 12

I apologize for the somewhat solemn, if not missionary, tones of the last letter. However, I would perhaps not be writing these lines if life around us proceeded more smoothly and was humanly satisfying. Let me close this "practical" part of our letters on a more joyful note, then, by introducing the happy sound of violins and cellos under the direction of a music teacher who is one of many who intuitively put into practice what we are attempting to analyze here in a more explicit fashion. Asked about his method of introducing violin music to grade-school children in an environment where string instruments are not yet known, he began by saying, "No textbook or method is successful and valuable unless it offers a basis for motivation. Our method takes into account that children generally desire to participate in music-making as part of a group. The task of the group is made obvious and simple. From the beginning musical notation and terms are introduced as part of a game. The children do not view these things as something extraneous and special, apart from playing the instrument."

The teacher continued by pointing out that in the very first lessons the children play music together, starting with simple rhythmic patterns and musical interactions

139

between various groups of players. The young student, as part of the group, applies the correct rhythm because if he did not, he would find himself outside the group. Moverover, the young player's imagination is encouraged by his being asked to construct and write down patterns consisting first of rhythmic notes and rests and later of simple melodies. These musical phrases are then played by the composer together with the entire group. He thus becomes aware of his active part in the shaping of the group's musical experience. Without his specific voice there would be something missing in the collaborative music that is being constructed. This makes each child conscious of the importance of his contribution.

When I hear a teacher express himself in such words and then observe how well this method is suited to the growing personality of the young child, I am greatly encouraged in my present attempt to make clear to teachers what does and what does not encourage the budding intelligence of these young children. The remarkable thing, of course, is that we do not usually connect musical skill with intellectual development. And, as you can guess, this music program, though regarded highly in the school district, was still considered an extracurricular activity, something of a luxury next to the traditional disciplines of an elementary school.

You said to me once before that the concept of intelligence which I propose is really quite close to what other people call "creativity." Although creativity is usually related to specific personality characteristics rather than primarily to intelligence, I would not hesitate to equate intelligence and creativity, because in Piaget's view intelligence is identical with development, with a going beyond present structures and an active transformation of present situational data. I have consistently suggested that our traditional view of intelligence is too limited in scope and impoverished by its failure to integrate intrinsic motivation. The purpose of the elementary grades should be to provide a setting in which intelligence, understood in Piaget's broad sense, is encouraged and rewarded. My reason for mentioning what this music teacher is doing—apart from my own love of music —is to show you how the opportunity can be given to children to express facets of their personalities that go along with their developing intelligence in the medium of music. To play in rhythm, to control intonation and intensity of tone, to construct musical phrases over time, and to symbolize all these things in musical notation, as well as to interact with others and submit one's activity to the group task—

all this is part and parcel of human intelligence. It is for this reason that the music teacher can justifiably rely on intrinsic motivation. His goal is musical thinking, with the accent on thinking. He is not concerned with turning every child into a professional violinist or musician. This would require, besides an ordinary structure of developed intelligence, special talents, interests, and environmental opportunities.

There is no doubt in my mind that other forms of creative art are just as suitable and wholesome for the young child. A school system that focuses on thinking will not neglect any of the ordinary media in which men express their intelligence constructively.

We realize that the use of "leisure" time is becoming a serious national problem. On this account alone schools can be expected to provide a foundation for activities that do not produce income or scholastic degrees but are as close to expressing what is best in human life as is science or social cooperation. Let me outline for you how the music teacher encouraged musical thinking and why this kind of activity is appropriate for the young child and contributes to his intellectual development.

The first lesson proceeded as follows. Twelve children from grades three and four came into the room, eight children carrying violins, four carrying cellos. The children sat down and listened as the teacher and another musician played some lively short pieces. "Would you like to play like this?" the teacher asked. He then promised the eager children that before this lesson was over, they would play music together.

The children then grouped the chairs so that each pair of children faced a music stand. They were shown how to hold the instrument with the left hand. (The bow is not used during the initial lessons.) They exercised as a group, lifting the instrument, putting it down, and holding it in playing position. The teacher showed them how to pluck the open A string and explained that in music one note follows the other, as do the beats of the heart or the steps of walking feet. And then the music started. The teacher took the instrument and plucked the A in the strict rhythm of four beats. He urged the children to follow him. Together they played four bars of four beats. The music notation was directly in front of the performing children; the five lines, the key, the bars, the notes. Everything was real, as in real music-making.

The children were now ready for an important step. The teacher crossed out the first note in each bar for the violins and in its place put the wavy line of a rest, whereas for the cellos he left the first note, but crossed out the following three notes to be replaced by three rests. Now the first beat was plucked by the four cellists and the remaining beats belonged to the eight violinists. This sequence continued for four bars. When the children were playing confidently, the teacher started improvising a melody over the rhythmic plucking of the children. Is there any child who would not be delighted with this musical performance? Perhaps I should ask the other rhetorical question. Is there any child at this age level who would be incapable of making music?

In the second lesson children were asked to write down different rhythms where the plucked notes were divided between the cellos (C) and the violins (V). Here are some of the rhythms which the children made up: CVCV, CVVC, VVCC. The teacher then introduced the piano and forte signs as well as crescendo ($<$) and decrescendo ($>$). With the help of these signs, the four-or eight-bar musical phrases were played with different dynamic characters—soft to loud, or soft-crescendo-loud-decrescendo-soft.

In subsequent lessons a second open string, D, was employed and the children's imagination produced many interesting phrases, such as the following:

This particular phrase started very softly and gradually became louder, ending with a thunderous D.

Eventually all four open strings were introduced, and the children realized that the cello and the violin each had one string peculiar to the instrument. So far each rhythmic beat was played either by both or by one of the instruments. Now, for the first time, general rests were introduced; that is, all players were quiet and silently rested for a specific number of beats. The first general rests were for a whole bar. After this came quarter-note rests with rhythms like 1-2-rest-4 or 1-2-3-rest.

Music classes met only twice a week. At the beginning of the fourth week, all children had developed a good sense of rhythm. At this time the teacher showed them how to beat rhythm and conduct the ensemble in playing together. Until now they had always played four beats to a bar (4/4). Now they learned three, two, and even five beats. In addition, eighth notes were added to the already familiar quarter notes. While the cellos plucked a string in quarter notes, the violins plucked in eighth notes. Then the roles were reversed, and eventually more difficult combinations were attempted. In all this playing the performance was constantly controlled by written signs. The child matched a musical notation (a symbol) with a concrete sound (reality), not unlike the symbol thinking we discussed in Letter 8.

After that the use of the bow was introduced. The handling of the bow was explained to the children as a function of the position of the instrument. With the bow it became possible to play whole, half, and three-quarter notes, and the appropriate symbols were accordingly introduced. After two lessons in which the children bowed on open strings, they began to use the fingers of the left hand to produce new tones. The teacher explained that the fingers worked like stoppers or hammers. To help with intonation, a piece of tape was put a whole tone above the open string to indicate the position of the first finger.

The teacher told me that from then onward the little musicians started playing songs and pieces, covering the entire range of notes in the first position. They were constantly in demand to perform for others, particularly parents and school administrators. This need to "justify the program and show results" interfered somewhat with the immediate goal of making music. Rehearsals for the concerts limited the possibilities for letting the children experiment with original melodies or combinations. The teacher also suggested that three meetings a week should be the minimum, because the children did not take their instruments home to practice. However, success of this string program was evident, as could be seen by its popularity among the children and its obvious accomplishments.

After being in the program for two years, the children were secure in the basic skills of being musicians. This meant intelligent control of behavior with the musical instrument according to the visually written and aurally interpreted requirement of the task, together with constant attention to the needs of the group. Such a task is in itself rewarding and supportive of the child's healthy development. If there were any aesthetic considerations, they were not a direct aim and were never the topic of lengthy discussion. The children were good sight readers and played as part of the group. They learned to correct an occasional mistake by listening to others and coming in at the appropriate place without interrupting the ensemble. They were familiar with more than one instrument and more than one key. When some children later transferred to playing the viola or the bass, they were remarkably quick at getting used to the alto clef or to different strings.

Asked about special talent, the teacher was not sure that any of the two hundred children he worked with had any outstanding predisposition. He thought it unlikely that any of them would become professional violinists. But what kind of education would aim primarily at the exceptional? We teach mathematics and history without expecting our children to become mathematicians or historians. Likewise, the children in this Virginia town played music because they were ordinary human beings. The teacher was sure that *any* children from any other environment would enjoy such a program and benefit from participating in it. Moreover, he had no doubt that the lives of these rural children had been permanently enriched even if they did not continue actively with music in subsequent school years.

As I listened to the string orchestra and observed the enthusiasm of the children and the audience, I too realized that for the children these were not trivial, secondary activities. Active participation in a constructive group task is the kind of food the human child needs in his growth toward maturity. Here the school encourages an active attitude toward enjoyment of music on which the child can draw in future years. For many adults, musical enjoyment is merely a passive experience of sound configurations which make an emotionally soothing background to an uninteresting activity. Such is the static, figurative knowing we described in previous letters. In contrast, the music teacher here knew how to engage operative knowing toward music and in addition provided an example of what good teaching is all about.

Sincerely yours,

one hundred and eighty school days of thinking

LETTER 13

I will now attempt to summarize the main ideas of our correspondence and to answer some of the questions that have been on your mind for some time, particularly the crucial question: How will all this fit together to make a school and fill a school day? In addition, I would like to take up a few loose ends and say a few words about such weighty educational topics as curriculum, testing, IQ, research, and early reading.

Here are the main facts as I see them. A child of elementary school age is capable of operative, intelligent thinking years ahead of his spoken language. More dramatically, the thinking of this child is light years ahead of what he can read or write. Traditionally, the response to this observation was: Teach him reading and writing so that he can express and expand his thinking. In Piaget's perspective the answer is: Strengthen his thinking so that the child will develop to the point where he can use the verbal medium intelligently. These are not merely opposing views of the focus of elementary school activities; within Piaget's framework, the traditional view is simply false. Language never expands thinking, if expansion means a more intelligent use of language. Thinking grows by means of formal abstraction from the general coordinations of actions, not from language. The child entering

145

school has barely attained the concrete operational stage. This means that he is beginning to have firm and stable general concepts (operations) which he can apply to *concrete* situations. By continuously and actively using his thinking structures within the expanding physical and social world in which he lives, the growing child between the ages of 11 and 13 reaches the stage of *formal* operational intelligence. Only then, and not before, is he capable of using verbal (formal) propositions as a challenge to this thinking.

The school for thinking that I propose will therefore relegate reading to an elective activity that will be encouraged but never imposed. Instead, my school will put all its emphasis on providing an environment in which the intelligence of the child can grow. This emphasis has nothing to do with the unfortunate preoccupation of "boosting the IQ." In a way, it is quite contrary to this notion. The school for thinking is in fact very little interested in measured IQ because it proposes to do what is uniformly beneficial to all. By its activities the school will recognize any extraordinary weaknesses or deficiencies in a child, and, if need be, it can refer him for special educational treatment. But the majority of normal individual differences in any given area will be taken care of in the course of the school's own program. A slight perceptual difficulty, which in the traditional reading school could lead to a potentially serious retardation in reading, will be observed early in visual thinking exercises and could be remedied through these activities. A more advanced child won't be held back; he will have plenty of opportunities to work to the limit of his capacity. Moreover, as I pointed out before, no constructive activity will be eliminated, especially if the child spontaneously asks for it; on the contrary, individual initiative would be constantly encouraged and a child who enjoyed reading would be given the opportunity to do so.

The purpose of the school for thinking, therefore, is to provide the setting in which the child's natural intelligence can develop to the fullest. Such a school is in no particular hurry about the development. No amount of time and reward by itself will make a person take in the tremendous amount of potential knowledge that is available unless he has the firm foundation of a mature and active intelligence. Grade schools can do no better service than to equip children with an eager capacity to apply their intelligence to whatever topic may be presented. Moreover, even in the traditional curriculum, the substantive content of what is learned during the six elementary grades is really quite meager and could be acquired in a short span of time by a well-motivated 12-year-old youngster who is used to thinking.

A school for thinking is not only suitable for the black child from the inner city, for the child from the Indian reservation, and for the child of migrant Mexican laborers, but also for the child from suburbia. The simple reason for this *equal opportunity* is that the school focuses on what is strongest in all children—their inner motivation to develop—rather than the one aspect in which, by arbitrary environmental selection, some sectors of our population are weaker or stronger than others. Yet this does not mean that even our schools for the white middle class are really successful. All it does mean is that these children could take the curriculum of the customary school without, apparently, being harmed by it. If thinking during elementary grades did develop, this was due primarily not to the school activities but to the general environment. And the general unrest and alienation of a large proportion of college students should give any educator pause to reflect where things have gone wrong in these young people's lives. One more word about the "successful" middle-class child. The number of scholastic failures—reading failures—even in this group is not negligible, and each case represents a tragic hardship for the child and his parents.

A fruitful theory is usually confirmed by a multiplicity of data. Piaget's theory of operative intelligence suggests that reading verbal material cannot be a challenging operative activity until the child's intelligence is close to formal operational intelligence. At earlier levels, reading is primarily what I have called a figurative skill, focusing on static written symbols as such rather than on the challenging content of the written material. Piaget's theoretical implications about the indirect role of linguistic skills in the early development of intelligence agree strikingly with psychological observations my colleagues and I collected in our years of research with linguistically deficient deaf children. Additional confirmation is now being provided in physiological evidence about the use of vision.

Dr. D.B. Harmon, a pioneer in the field of perceptual-motor development, suggested to me the other day that physiologically, too, it is inappropriate to stress *near* vision until the visual system approaches full development and that for its development it needs the active use of *far* vision. We talked about visual defects that are increasingly observed in grade schools, particularly in the case of children with reading difficulties. He was of the opinion, shared by many optometrists, that most of these defects are not so much the cause of reading difficulties as the result of early learning that was physiologically unsound. In other words, when a young child experiences stress in connection with having to learn to read (in order to live up to what is expected of him), this psychological stress reinforces the already existing physiological stress (due to near vision activity). Later on, the functioning of the child's visual system will be found to be faulty, and visual training will be recommended to undo the harm of earlier learning; this rehabilitation sometimes succeeds dramatically. Suppose, when a young child is learning to play the piano, that you observe stiffness in all his fingers right up to the shoulders; if you want him to become a halfway successful pianist, the first thing to do is to tell him to stop playing. In the same way, stressful close visual work in early reading is harmful; when it becomes obvious, a sensitive teacher should be able to tell the child, "Stop reading."

In accordance with this view Dr. Harmon did a carefully controlled experiment in which two groups of children entering first grade were equated. Both groups were treated exactly alike except that one group started formal reading instruction after one month in school, and the other was given visual thinking games but no formal instruction in reading until mid-year. At the end of the school year the two groups were indistinguishable in reading skill. This result, surprising at first, is really not so startling. We know that illiterate adults in underdeveloped countries have little difficulty in learning to read if they are well motivated and if appropriate reading material is available to them.

We must recognize that reading and intelligence are different psychological phenomena; the dependency of reading on intelligence is different from the dependency of intelligence on reading. Reading first requires the figurative ability to comprehend an arbitrary symbolic code, and this ability begins to be evident in the preoperational period of symbol formation. Consequently, it is no miracle that a three- or four-year-old child can read some words. Second, reading increasingly requires the operative ability to comprehend verbal propositions. Note that the language of books is different from the spoken language, primarily because the spoken word is part of an ongoing dialogue in a concrete situation whereas written sentences that are intellectually challenging take on the form of propositions. The ability to master propostions is not fully developed until the formal operational period. Thus, between the ages of 11 and 13 reading and thinking can join together and expand the intellect of the reader. Not knowing how to read becomes potentially harmful to the intellect at the formal period but is of no particular consequence for the developing intelligence at earlier ages. This is an interesting parallel to the well known fact that the onset of speech may vary by the relatively huge span of a year and a half, between nine months and 27 months, without having any definite relation to the intelligence of the infant.

You ask me explicitly how children would learn to read in the thinking school. They would learn it when they showed spontaneous interest in books. The teacher would encourage the child's interest by reading from books, by writing during other activities, by exposing him to rhythmic and poetic qualities of language, and so on. She would use some of the excellent self-training materials on the market today, but without pushing him. If the child shows interest, there is every reason to think that he is ready and will succeed. Success in learning reading means this: the child exposed to the figurative material can spontaneously discover (that is, is sufficiently interested to discover) the coding rules; he need not labor to "remember" the rules and can enjoy the content. Thus, reading becomes potentially open to operative thinking about the content. But what if the child does not show any interest? I find it hard to imagine a child in our society who, if consistently encouraged for one, two, or three years to apply his operative thinking, would fail to show interest in reading. Besides, the children I am talking about have not had the crippling experience of failing in reading. It is quite a different matter to give remedial instruction to a nine-year-old child who has to overcome past failures than to guide a child of similar age who, after successful and satisfying scholastic experience, takes up reading as a fresh topic.

The school for thinking would not be tied to any fixed curriculum. Think of the freedom and initiative that could result from this fortunate condition. There would be no need for completing a fixed assignment but ample time to focus on the essential development. I know quite well that these are the last years in a child's life that such a luxury is appropriate. If by the end of his fourth year in elementary school a child had learned nothing else than to use his intellect in the ordinary activities of his life and to apply his intellect while reading, would this not be a very desirable result, and one that augurs well for future learning? There would be no division into reading groups, or at least no more division in reading than in other activities. And the stress would be on the other activities. Instead of classifying and evaluating children according to the alien standards of reading or IQ, the children would group themselves naturally according to their own level of intellectual development.

A school like this, of course, does not simply happen. Yet it is by no means an impossible dream. It could happen tomorrow in your school district and others if administrators, teachers, and parents would get together and seriously consider the task of early education. A school for thinking can only function in a school system and a social environment in which the concern is with the child, not with extraneous personal, social, or political motives. There must be a spirit of mutual cooperation and an atmosphere of trust and initiative. I think such a state of affairs is easier to create when everyone recognizes that the child's developing intelligence is the chief factor in the game—not a certain skill which the adult has to impose on the child. Teachers rightly complain of feeling exhausted at the end of a school day, for they seem to be constantly on the giving end, handing out the questions and imposing the answers. We teachers would feel much more creative if we saw our role as coach or guide rather than as dispenser of goods. I think that an unsuitable theory of development and learning has stifling effects not only on classroom teaching but also on the mutual relations of teachers, administrators, and parents.

I was glad to read that you and your colleagues realize the difference between curriculum and structure. I am certainly not in favor of an unstructured educational program in which children do as they please. On the contrary, the structural change I have in mind implies a structured setting through which the children's intelligence is challenged. My stand against a fixed curriculum is not based on objections to any particular topic; rather, I fear that emphasizing content easily leads to the imposition of figurative, low-level operative knowing. This works to the detriment of the high-level operative activity that is necessary food for the growing intelligence.

When I sketch in the following paragraphs what a day's activity could be like, I will refer mainly to examples described earlier and illustrate how these could be used in a school program. You should have no difficulty in introducing other activities that have been demonstrated to stimulate the child's intelligence.

For children of six and seven the school day starts at 9:00 a.m. with a story, something interesting and beautiful that includes poetry, songs, and action. From 9:20 to 10:00 the children keep busy with visual thinking games, in particular with matching, reversal, and hidden-figure games. From 10:00 to 10:40 they visit the nearby grocery store and observe some of the things that go on behind the scenes —unloading of trucks, storing, distribution. There are three groups of about eight children, each focusing on some grocery operation. They ask questions and take pictures. Each group brings back to school some goods that the store hands out to the children. After a recess the class continues from 11:00 to 11:40 with discussion and evaluation of the visit to the store. Each group in turn acts out scenes about the store activity observed. From 11:40 to noon there are physical exercises, particularly those that require coordination and balance.

After lunch the class divides into three groups to engage in handicrafts, art, and music. These assignments change from day to day so that each child is exposed to all three activities. From 1:40 to 2:00 is another short period for listening to an interesting story or continuing the story started at the beginning of the day. Then follows another short period of physical exercises (2:00–2:15) and a second short period of thinking games (2:15–2:30), perhaps the probability game described in letter 9. Finally, from 2:30 to 3:00 the children gather around the goods they brought from the store and cook them, divide them, eat them, or take some home.

A class that is about two years older may spend a school day like this. From 9:00 to 9:20 a story is read to them; it includes some poetry selections and group recitation of poetry. Symbol-picture logic follows at 9:20. From 9:40 to 11:40 there is dramatic play, with tug-of-war and part-whole. The class divides into three groups; one acts while the others make up the audience. After each group's activity there is a lively evaluation. This class foregoes its recess time —acting is in itself fun and recreational—and after a period of physical exercise (11:40–noon) is free for lunch. From 1:00 to 1:40 there is a period devoted to visual thinking games. The class breaks up into smaller groups, each group doing some task according to its wish. A number of children work alone and some engage in reading. From 1:40 to 2:30 is an excursion to a nearby post office, and, as usual, three groups observe different activities. Each group collects some written material, whether it be some postal regulations, a piece of mail, or a blank form. Back in the classroom, they have a pertinent discussion about their observations and the material they brought along. The teacher writes on the board some of the important topics and finally helps the children come to some general conclusions.

The school for thinking on which we have focused throughout our correspondence is limited to the first three or four elementary grades. This is done because at the age of grade five a child can begin to be exposed to specific topics, whereas our primary concern is the laying of a secure foundation. Naturally, we would like to see the emphasis on thinking continued in higher grades, and some changes in the system of teaching are desirable—indeed, are needed—right up to the graduate school. But if changes are to be effective, I can think of no more important period for starting these changes than the first grades of elementary school. Experience has already amply demonstrated that preschool education cannot inoculate a child against the psychological harm of the traditional system. Intervention at a later grade level invariably risks being remedial, that is, undoing some earlier harm, or coming too late and leaving out large masses of children who simply could not make it at all.

I would like to stress the relative "cheapness" of my suggested program. Almost no special expenses would be required—only, perhaps, some additional teaching aides to help with the youngest children. In addition, wherever possible, I would equip classrooms not with heavy desks but simply with chairs that can be arranged in any order or moved out of the way according to need.

If I were asked to initiate such a program, I would insist that the children and the teachers be freed from the *outside* pressure of being tested and evaluated until the end of the third or fourth year of school. This requirement is simply a gesture of self-defense against the scientific-looking methodology prevalent in our research in education and social science. We cannot expect that our teachers, our parents, and our children can launch on a new adventure if the standards derived from old methods are constantly being applied to them. I do not want a teacher or a parent to get nervous when his seven-year-old child does not show interest in reading. Apart from this, there will, of course, be a constant *internal* evaluation as part of the program, since the teacher observes each child and obtains a rich picture of his activity.

The programs I described in Part Two of our letters are now considered luxury items, added to the ordinary program and financed by outside money, and are in danger of being dropped when the outside source stops funding. All these programs have a constant battle to fight and must justify their existence. We are so consumer-minded that we invariably fall back on immediate results. Unless we see the score on some achievement test rising with each school year, we are not satisfied. Moreover, we hide our shortsightedness under the cloak of scientific respectability. Thus research becomes a frantic search for immediate results that pass the magical barrier of statistical significance.

What happens to the real child in the meantime? Who knows whether the physical exercises he does during the grade school years will enable him to remain a healthy, strong adult once he is past 60? Who knows whether the accepting attitude of the elementary school will help him to withstand a personal upheaval at age 45 which could ruin an emotionally less healthy individual? Who knows whether the thinking activities which the child enjoyed during his early school years can provide the spark that at age 25 turns a floundering career into constructive channels? Who knows whether the social interests awakened during the early grades keep smoldering until they burst out in the young man or woman who decides to devote his life to the well-being of his fellow men?

I know that change is hard and that all kinds of arguments can be brought against any change, not the least of which is that whatever is proposed as a change hasn't yet been tried. And since it has not been tried, we do not know whether it will work. Ergo . . . no change.

On many occasions books and articles have called for educational reform, and education has continued on its way, largely unaffected by these calls for change. New methods of teaching specific topics appear constantly, and many relevant and desirable things are in fact suggested and exemplified. Unfortunately, as these good ideas filter down to the ordinary classroom teacher who must still work within the traditional system, the difference between the new and the old methods of teaching often becomes imperceptible. I have, however, purposefully gone out of my way to make sure that the proposed school for thinking is not primarily regarded as just a new method of teaching. Instead, I have proposed Piaget's theory of intelligence as a new base on which to build the educational treatment of the child.

I should not be at all surprised, in fact, if some teacher told you that many of her present school activities are quite similar to what I have suggested here. For this teacher it should be of some benefit to know that Piaget's work on operational intelligence provides a firm scientific foundation for her daily activities. The same holds true with regard to the various new programs that are employed throughout the country and that stress the thinking process rather than the content of a particular curriculum.

Once we comprehend what thinking and its development is all about, we can constructively argue about specific methods and exact details. I have no desire to impose my examples as definitive or necessarily the best possible ones. I have simply tried to show you some ways in which you can put the new perspective on intelligence into practice. You, the teacher, in constant touch with the children, are the final judge of what can or cannot be done in a classroom. I am looking forward to cooperating with you and to learning from your experience.

My best wishes, and let me hear from you.

Sincerely yours,

for further reading

Almy, M. *Young children's thinking: studies of some aspects of Piaget's theory.* New York: Teachers College Press, 1966.

Athey, I.J., and D.O. Rubadeau (eds.). *Educational implications of Piaget's theory: a book of readings.* Waltham, Mass.: Blaisdell, 1970.

Beard, Ruth Mary. *An outline of Piaget's developmental psychology for students and teachers.* New York: Basic Books, Inc., 1969.

Boyle, D.G. *A students' guide to Piaget.* Elmsford, N.Y.: Pergamon Press, 1969.

Elkind, D. *Children and adolescents: interpretative essays on Jean Piaget.* New York: Oxford University Press, 1970.

Furth, H. G. *Thinking without language: psychological implications of deafness.* New York: The Free Press, 1966.

————. *Piaget and knowledge: theoretical foundations.* Englewood Cliffs, N.J.: Prentice-Hall, Inc., 1969.

Ginsburg, H., and S. Opper. *Piaget's theory of intellectual development: An Introduction.* Englewood Cliffs, N.J.: Prentice-Hall, Inc., 1969.

Piaget, J. *Six psychological studies.* New York: Random House, Inc., 1968.

Piaget, J., and B. Inhelder. *The psychology of the child.* New York: Basic Books, Inc., 1969.

Ripple, R. E., and V. N. Rockcastle (eds.). Piaget rediscovered. In Papers from a Conference on Cognitive Studies and Curriculum Development, *Journal of research in science teaching,* 1964, 2, 3.

Sinclair, H., and C. Kamii. Some implications of Piaget's theory for teaching young children. In *School review,* 1970, 78.

glossary

Abstraction, formal, reflecting— Feedback from the coordinating or operational activities to the interior organization which enables it to "reflect" on the general form of the activities. Formal, reflecting abstraction is the principal source of the growth of intelligence as general, logical knowledge.

Abstraction, physical—Feedback from the result of actions on physical objects or qualities. Physical abstraction presupposes the framework of formal abstraction and leads to critical, objective knowledge of the physical world.

Accommodation—The outgoing process of an operative action oriented toward some particular reality state. Accommodation applies a general structure to a particular situation; as such, it always contains some element of newness. In a restricted sense, accommodation to a new situation leads to the differentiation of a previous structure and thus the emergence of new structures.

Action—A functional exchange between a biological organization and the environment that presupposes an internal structure and leads to a structuring of the environment. For Piaget, action is not limited to external action. It is generally synonymous with behavior.

Adaptation—A balanced state of a biological organization within its

157

environment. In behavior, an equilibration between assimilation and accommodation.

Affectivity—The aspect of behavior that has to do with interest, motivation, dynamics, energy. It is indissociably linked to the structural aspect of knowing.

Assimilation—The incorporating process of an operative action. A taking in of environmental data, not in a causal, mechanistic sense, but as a function of an internal structure that by its own nature seeks activity through assimilation of potential material from the environment.

Centration—In perception, the focusing on a specific part of a stimulus; in general, a subjective focusing on an aspect of a given situation leading to a deformation of objectivity.

Concept—In a logical sense, a mental construct of the generalizable aspect of a known thing; it has an intension (or comprehension) answering the question, "What is its essence?" and an extension answering the question as to which things are exemplars of the concept. In a psychological sense, a concept is identical with an individual's internal structure or scheme and corresponds to the level of that structure (e.g., "practical" concept). In its verbal manifestations, concept is a verbalized expression of a logical concept together with its verbalized comprehension; however, verbalization is extrinsic to the logical concept as such.

Concrete operation—Characteristic of the first stage of operational intelligence. A concrete operation implies underlying general systems or "groupings" such as classification, seriation, number. Its applicability is limited to objects considered as real (concrete).

Conservation—The maintenance of a structure as invariant during physical changes of some aspects. The stability of an objective attribute is never simply given, it is constructed by the living organization. Conservation therefore implies an internal system of regulations that can compensate internally for external changes.

Coordination—The functional adaptation or the unifying form of the elements of an action, particularly of an external action though not limited to it; implies an active internal structure.

Empiricism—A philosophical opinion that holds that all knowledge including necessary logical truth has its adequate and sufficient cause in information that derives ultimately from the senses; it assumes that objectivity is simply "out there" and veridically given.

Epistemology—The theoretical science concerning the nature of knowledge, in particular of scientific knowledge and of necessary logical truth; usually considered a branch of philosophical inquiry. For Piaget, epistemology is a problem open to scientific, particularly psychological, investigation.

Equilibration—The internal regulatory factor underlying a biological organization; it is manifested in all life, particularly in the development and activity of intelligence. Intelligence makes explicit the regulations inherent in an organization. As a process, it is the regulatory factor that unifies evolution and development; as a state (an equilibrium), it is a continuously changing balancing of active compensations.

Field effects—Perceptual phenomena occurring during a single centration of the sense organ. They can be considered as the momentary limit of perceptual activities.

Figurative knowledge—Knowledge that focuses on the external, figural aspect of an event in a static manner, closely tied to a particular accommodation as illustrated in perception, imitation, image, memory. Figurative knowledge is conceivable only within a framework of operative knowing.

Formal operation—Typically manifested in propositional thinking and a combinatory system that considers the real as one among other hypothetical possibilities. Formal operations are characteristic of the second and final stage of operational intelligence which "reflects" on concrete operations through the elaboration of formal "group" structures.

Image—The internal representation of an external event. The image is one of the products of the symbolic function, hence of intelligence in its total functioning; it is not a mere trace from passive perception.

Imitation—The figurative correspondence of motor activity to an external event. Imitation has three stages: (1) sensory-motor imitation, identical with perceptual accommodation, (2) deferred imitation (gesture) in the absence of the model, the beginning of symbol formation, (3) internalized imitation, the image.

Innate—Present at birth or conception. "Innate" is frequently opposed to "learned," yet evolutionary learning is as true a learning as developmental acquisition. Innate behavior patterns are called instincts.

Intelligence—In the wide sense, the totality of possible coordinations that structure the behavior of an organism. Intelligence considered as a totality characterizes a given stage and is derived from the actual coordinations of a previous stage through formal reflecting abstraction. In a narrower sense, it is limited to operational intelligence, including sometimes the later stages of the sensory-motor period.

Interiorization—The eventual dissociation between the general form of a coordination and the particular content of an external action. Interiorization leads from "practical" to operational intelligence and is the precondition for objective knowledge as well as for symbolic representation.

Internalization—The eventual diminution of external movements that become covert and sketchy, illustrated in imitation and language. Internalization leads to internal symbols; to be differentiated from interiorization. Piaget commonly uses the one French word *intériorisation* for both interiorization and internalization. English writers use both words interchangeably while meaning internalization.

Knowledge—The structuring of behavior as interchange between organism and environment. Behavior at every level implies a certain amount of knowedge on the part of the organism concerning the environment. General objective knowledge is identical with intelligence.

Language—The natural spoken (and heard) symbol system of communication typical of a society. One of the manifestations of symbol functioning. Language is acquired and used like other symbol behavior and chiefly influences intelligence indirectly through the social, educative impact of society.

Learning—In the strict sense, acquisition of knowledge due to some particular information provided by the environment. Learning is inconceivable without a theoretically prior interior structure of equilibration which provides the capacity to learn and the structuring of the learning process; in the wide sense, it includes both factors.

Logic—As a formalized system, can be employed to describe the structuring spontaneously manifest in intelligent behavior. The internal consistency and necessity of logical judgments command our intellectual assent. There is a continuous genetic relation between mature logical forms and prelogical structures of early behavior.

Logical positivism—A philosophical opinion that holds that logic and abstract intelligence are heavily dependent on the correct formalization and use of language. Logical positivism is a modification of empiricism, which emphasizes language as the source of logical intelligence.

Maturation—Biological changes as a function of increasing age in the anatomical and physiological system, insofar as they determine behavioral development.

Memory—In the strict sense, active knowledge that refers to a particular past; image evocation and recognition do not by themselves imply memory. In the wide sense, memory is the availability of any knowledge and merely expresses the fact that the conservation of a scheme is identical with the functioning of the scheme.

Object Formation—The scheme of the permanent object is the first most general invariant that constitutes initial objectivation, the presence of a thing "out there" independent of the child's own actions. The environment does not by itself provide objectively given reality. Object formation stands at the threshold of operational intelligence.

Operation—In the strict sense, the characteristic interiorized generalizable action of mature intelligence; an operation implies a structure through which: (1) the resulting "knowing" need not be exteriorized as in sensorimotor intelligence, and (2) an operation is reversible—it can turn in an inverse direction and thus negate its own activity. In the wide sense, operational is here taken to include preoperational but exclude sensorimotor actions.

Operativity—Contrasted with figurative knowledge it implies the action aspect of intelligence at all periods, including sensorimotor intelligence. Operativity is the essential, generalizable structuring aspect of intelligence insofar as knowing means constructing, transforming, incorporating, etc.

Organization—The most general expression of the form of a biological organism, a totality in which elements are related to each other and to the whole, the totality itself being related to a greater totality. The functioning of the organism gives content to the organization. All biological phenomena including intelligence and evolution find their basic explanation in the biological organization. An organization has intrinsic regulatory mechanisms.

Perception—A knowing activity that is focused on the immediately given sensory data.

Perceptual activity—Regulations of sense organs during perception; a coordinating of successive centrations. Perceptual activities usually compensate for the momentary deformations of centration, thus are part of operative, more specifically sensorimotor intelligence.

Play—As a symbolic instrument, play expresses the knowing of the child who uses things or gestures in a symbolic manner, that is, not adapted to their proper function but assimilated to the child's ego-motivated representational activity.

Preoperational—Often used to designate the period after the sensorimotor stage but prior to the formation of the first operations in the strict sense. The preoperational period is the preparatory part of the stage of concrete operational intelligence, characterized by the deforming need for symbolic support, hence egocentrism.

Representation—In the strict sense, "to represent" means "to make present something not present"; e.g., as in an image or symbolic play. In a somewhat inappropriate and misleading sense, "representational" is attributed to knowledge above the sensorimotor stage, insofar as it is no longer exclusively tied to external acts.

Reversibility—The possibility of performing a given action in a reversed direction. Its two chief forms are negation (not male=female) and reciprocity (not better=worse). Reversibility is the criterion of an underlying operational structure.

Scheme—The internal general form of a specific knowing activity, frequently, but not exclusively, used for sensorimotor intelligence. The generalizable aspect of coordinating actions that can be applied to analogous situations. Operations are nothing but the most general schemes of operational intelligence. Schemes are coordinated among themselves in higher-order structures or schemes. (Piaget distinguishes scheme from the term "schema," which conveys a representational outline, a figurative model. Schema is related to a figurative accommodation or symbol; scheme, to operativity.)

Sensorimotor—The characteristic mode of knowledge of the first stage of intelligence in which the form of knowledge is tied to the content of specific sensory input or motoric actions. Also referred to as practical intelligence.

Sign (signifier, significate)—An event that takes the place of another event as evidenced by its behavioral effect. A sign is a signifier and as such indicates another event called significate. Sign behavior falls into two distinct categories according to whether the organism reacts to the sign as a signal or as a symbol.

Signal—A signal is a substitute stimulus to which the organism reacts without differentiating the signifying sign from the significate.

Hence, it is an undifferentiated part of a global situation and the reaction is to the total situation, not to the signal as such. Sensorimotor intelligence corresponds to signal behavior, e.g., in conditioning, perceptual recognition, associative learning. A signal is also called an index.

Stages—Successive developmental periods of intelligence, each one characterized by a relatively stable general structure that incorporates developmentally earlier structures in a higher synthesis. The regular sequence of stage-specific activities is decisive for intellectual development rather than chronological age.

Structure—The general form, the interrelatedness of parts within an organized totality. Structure can often be used interchangeably with organization, system, form, coordination.

Symbol, symbolic function—A symbol is a sign that is differentiated from its significate. The symbolic function is the person's capacity to construct or produce a symbol for representing that which the person knows and which is not present. Consequently, any symbol, whether produced or comprehended, presupposes the constructive activity of operational thinking and depends on it; in turn, operations do not always require symbols. While a signal signifies the external event in an undifferentiated manner, the symbol signifies ("refers to") the thing-as-known. Piaget restricts the meaning of the word "sign" to linguistic or other conventional symbols and in contrast restricts the word "symbol" to an ego-involved signifier; he has recently renamed the symbolic function as the "semiotic function" in order to indicate that what he calls signs are also included in this function.

Thinking—Active intelligence or knowing, usually limited to operational (in the wide sense) activities.

Transformation—As external transformation, refers to the constantly changing appearance of the physical world. As internal transformation, refers to knowing as constructing invariants through which external changes can be internally compensated for. Operations are internal transformations relative to an invariant and consequently they lead to an objective understanding of physical changes.